CONTENTS

CO-AKI-100

From the Editor

Paul's Letter to the Galatians and its emphasis on grace is the focus of this January Bible Study. Many people in today's world misunderstand the nature of the gospel. Even some church attenders view salvation as adherence to the Ten Commandments. At the same time, church attenders appear to be selective when it comes to which Commandments they follow. Many believe sin that doesn't appear to impact others or is permissible in a court of law can be ignored.

Paul addressed both these issues in his Letter to the Galatians. The Galatian church was beginning to accept a false gospel, one that included adherence to the Mosaic law as necessary for salvation. Paul addressed the issue, defining salvation as God's grace realized through faith. Paul also balanced his presentation of salvation by grace by reminding believers that liberty doesn't give them license.

This Learner Guide is written in an informal, easy-to-read style that helps the reader understand the biblical text without extensive comments. It also has a series of helps to enhance each reader's study. Each chapter includes:

• LEARNING ACTIVITIES integral to the teaching plans included in the Leader Guide.

• At least one feature entitled A CLOSER LOOK that elaborates on or provides summary information on related chapter topics.

• Sets of questions entitled FOR YOUR CONSIDERATION. Some questions relate to Bible content, while some are application questions that help you focus on the passage's present-day meaning for your life. These questions can be used in individual or group study and with the Learning Activities can help a group leader stimulate discussion.

At the beginning of each chapter, you will find the BIBLE TRUTH and LIFE GOAL. The Bible Truth briefly states the main abiding spiritual principle for that chapter. The Life Goal identifies the main application we hope learners will take with them.

Dr. Argile Smith, pastor of First Baptist Church, Biloxi, Mississippi, wrote this Learner Guide. Dr. Smith is a graduate of William Carey College (B.A.) and New Orleans Baptist Theological Seminary (M.Div., Ph.D.).

WRITTEN BY
ARGILE SMITH

TRUTH *About* GRACE

STUDIES IN GALATIANS

LifeWay Press®
Nashville, TN

No part of this work may be reproduced or transmitted in any form or by any means, electronic or mechanical, including photocopying and recording, or by any information storage or retrieval system, except as may be expressly permitted in writing by the publisher. Requests for permission should be addressed in writing to LifeWay Press®, One LifeWay Plaza, Nashville, TN 37234-0173.

ISBN: 978-1-4158-6535-4
Item: 005146135

Subject Area: Bible Studies
Dewey Decimal Classification Number: 231.72
Subject Heading: TRUTH ABOUT GRACE: STUDIES IN GALATIANS
Printed in the United States of America

Leadership and Adult Publishing
LifeWay Church Resources
One LifeWay Plaza
Nashville, TN 37234-0175

We believe the Bible has God for its author; salvation for its end; and truth, without any mixture of error, for its matter and that all Scripture is totally true and trustworthy. The 2000 statement of The Baptist Faith and Message is our doctrinal guideline.

Unless otherwise indicated, all Scripture quotations are from the Holman Christian Standard Bible®, Copyright © 1999, 2000, 2002, 2003 by Holman Bible Publishers. Holman Christian Standard Bible®, Holman CSB®, and HCSB® are federally registered trademarks of Holman Bible Publishers.
Used by permission.

Cover Image: IStock Photo
Chapter Beginnings: IStock Photo
Lesson Photos: *Biblical Illustrator* Photos

Chapter 1
Galatians 1:1-24

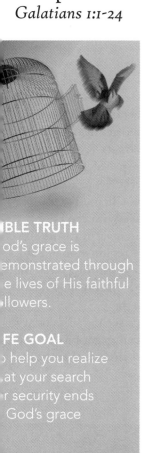

BLE TRUTH
od's grace is
emonstrated through
e lives of His faithful
llowers.

FE GOAL
help you realize
at your search
r security ends
God's grace

NO OTHER GOSPEL

N orma sat down at her computer and wiped the tears from her eyes. She sat there staring at the screen, and then she took a long breath, trying to exhale her exasperation. Then she sat there a little longer, glaring at the screen and wondering how things could have gone so wrong so quickly. Finally, she opened her e-mail account and addressed a message to her son, Greg.

Greg had just left for college a few weeks earlier. He had grown up in church, and nothing made him as happy as serving the Lord with the other youth in his church. When Greg went off to college, he got involved with Christian groups eager to grow in Christ together.

In his dormitory, however, he met Tim, a guy who led him to believe that he had been wrong. Claiming the Bible as his authority, Tim said that Jesus didn't really save anyone for eternity. Tim went on to insist that Jesus only saved us to give us another chance to live right. Of course, living right meant keeping some rules that Tim had identified from his misrepresentation of three or four obscure Bible passages.

Greg believed Tim's explanation. He sent his mother an e-mail message in which he explained the new insights Tim had shown him. He also told her about his decision to leave the way of simple faith in Christ and embrace the path Tim had shown him.

As Norma began to write her reply to Greg, her fingers trembled on the keypad. She struggled with two competing emotions: her disappointment with Greg and her anger toward Tim. Most of all, she ached over the misguided path Greg had taken.

Paul could have identified with Norma's sorrow. His letter to the Galatian Christians reveals his agony over the bad choices they had made with their liberty in Christ.

A Prelude (Gal. 1:1-5)

As Paul began his letter to the Galatian churches, his heart ached over the spiritual direction they had taken. The apostle had poured his heart into the churches there for years. He had met them on his first missionary journey when he passed through the Galatian region proclaiming the gospel of Jesus Christ (Acts 13-14). Pisidian Antioch, Iconium, Lystra, and Derbe were located in Galatia. Having led some of the people there to receive Christ, he planted churches and helped them get off to a good start in their walk with the Lord.

Paul's devotion to the Christians in Galatia had almost cost him his life. According to Acts 14:19, the opponents of the gospel in the region stoned Paul. They thought they had killed him, but he survived. Instead of running away for his own safety, he kept on preaching in the region, laying his life on the line for the sake of the Galatian churches.

Paul returned to the region on two other occasions. On his second missionary journey he made his way back to Galatia to check on the congregations he had established (Acts 16:1-6). He also spent some time with the believers there at the outset of his third missionary journey (Acts 18:23).

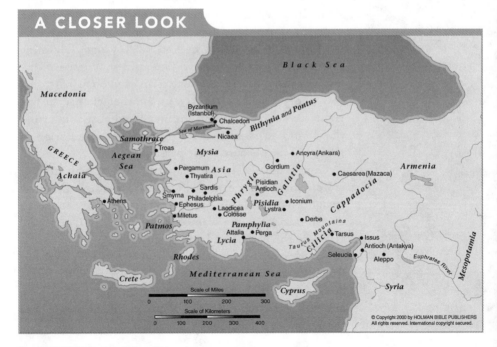

A CLOSER LOOK

© Copyright 2000 by HOLMAN BIBLE PUBLISHERS
All rights reserved. International copyright secured.

The Letter to the Galatians shows us the depth of Paul's love for believers and churches. His love prompted him to take action on their behalf by sending them a clear warning.

Paul's action serves as an excellent example for believers today in our relationships with one another. We have an obligation to nurture one another in Christ. Nurturing others can be hard work, but it's necessary if we intend to help one another as we serve Him together. When we warn other Christians about the challenges and temptations that lie ahead, we do something that can reap huge benefits in God's kingdom work.

In the introduction of his letter, Paul reminded the Galatian Christians of his calling as an apostle (1:1). He didn't want them to lose sight of the fact that God had sent him to their region years earlier to proclaim the gospel. Later in his letter he would have much more to say about his call to be an apostle and the gospel he proclaimed. In the introduction, however, he wanted to clarify his authority to address the problem facing them and stunting their spiritual growth.

Paul also referenced some unnamed companions who accompanied him (1:2). This probably included Barnabas (Acts 13:1). Paul's brothers in Christ served the Lord with him as partners in his missionary work. In that role they bore with him the burden for the churches. Consequently, they undoubtedly shared Paul's broken heart for the Galatian believers who would receive the apostle's letter.

As Paul greeted the Galatians, he mentioned grace and peace (1:3). These two key terms always appear together in the introductions of the letters Paul wrote. Grace involves everything God does for us through Jesus Christ even though we don't deserve it. Of course, the central and most profound expression of God's grace is in Jesus (1:4). Jesus' life, death, burial, and resurrection render for us who have received His gift of salvation a relationship with God we don't deserve. God's grace leads to our peace with Him.

Paul's statement about praising God should resonate with all believers everywhere. Our awareness of God's grace in Christ moves us to praise Him (1:5). Only God can save us from our sin. We can't earn the privilege of a relationship with Him, no matter how hard we may try.

Because of God's love for us, He took the initiative to provide the only way we could have a relationship with Him. Taking the initiative meant sending His Son to die as a sacrifice for our sin. When we think about the depth of His love for us and the expression of it in Christ, praise flows from our hearts and through our lips. With Paul, we give Him all the glory forever!

For Your Consideration

1. How did Paul become an apostle?

2. What's the connection between grace and peace?

3. Why is it crucial for you to have a firm understanding of God's grace in your life?

A Problem (Gal. 1:6-10)

By receiving Christ, we experience God's grace. Our sins have been forgiven. The wall separating us and God has come tumbling down, and an intimate relationship with Him has begun. Christ has liberated us from our slavery to sin. Nothing can compare with God's grace in setting us free to serve Him. For that reason we react in shock when a believer walks away from the liberating gospel of grace to attempt a different path.

We can understand, then, how much the news about the Galatians troubled Paul (1:6). On his most recent visit with them, the apostle had observed the pure joy in their hearts because they had received Christ and had grown in their walk with Him.

Not long after Paul left them, however, a terrible thing happened. Someone came along and began to deceive them with destructive teachings. The false instruction they received went against the grain of the gospel Paul had taught them. In fact, it had absolutely no resemblance of the gospel at all. Instead of prompting them to live out their liberty in Christ, the deceitful instruction condemned them to lives of spiritual slavery. Instead of growing in a meaningful relationship with the Lord, they would be destined to suffer spiritually under the heavy weight of legalism. Paul could hardly believe that they would have considered embracing something so contrary to the life-changing gospel he had preached to them.

The danger of legalism can never be underestimated. Legalism is a way of life in which a Christian reduces his or her walk with Christ to keeping a set of religious rules. Granted, a relationship with God requires us to live according to His ways. However, merely keeping religious rules can become a pitiful and sorry substitute for a lively walk with God.

Legalism is a way of life in which a Christian reduces his or her walk with Christ to keeping a set of religious rules.

That Paul would take such a strong stand against legalism makes sense to us. Instead of trusting the Lord with our lives and allowing Him to stretch us according to His plan for us, legalism directs us to develop a checklist of obligations. Legalistic religious duty involves nothing more than keeping the obligations on the checklist. Walking with the Lord by faith opens the door for fulfillment in life as He intended for us to experience it. By contrast, a religion of keeping rules alone closes the door on that kind of fulfillment. Such a life swirls around nothing more than scratching check marks on the wall of the prison in which legalism places us.

The path toward spiritual slavery taken by the Galatian Christians reminds us to pay close attention to the content of religious teaching. As in

Paul's day, we thank the Lord for sound Bible teachers. However, we sometimes may encounter teachers who offer deceptive instruction for Christians. At first these teachers may be convincing, but in time the heresy of their message will come to light.

The message we embrace as Christians involves the simple truth of salvation by grace through faith in Christ. Adding or taking away something from that simple truth always is deceptive and dangerous. According to Paul, teachers who lead Christians astray with deceptive instruction can expect to pay an awful price for their heresies. They will face the curse of God's judgment (1:8-9).

Calling attention to a dangerous message and a deceptive messenger may make us unpopular (1:10). That's a risk we must be willing to take. Our devotion to the Lord in gratitude for His grace may compel us to speak up when we see truth being elbowed out by deception. We have a responsibility to help one another stay on track, even if we run the risk of disturbing one another. When someone wanders away from living by simple faith in Christ and embraces teaching that's contrary to the gospel of grace, we are to call attention to it. When we help one another in that important way, we please God.

For Your Consideration

1. What is legalism, and why is it so attractive in our culture?

2. Why do Christians often tend to refrain from warning one another about false teachings and teachers?

3. What steps do you take to keep yourself from falling into doctrinal or spiritual deception?

Characteristics of Legalism

Match the characteristic on the left with its corresponding reference on the right.

1. Legalism tends to result in tumultuous human relationships.   a. Gal. 4:17
2. Legalism results in a joyless religious faith.   b. Gal. 5:9
3. Legalism demonstrates misguided enthusiasm.   c. Gal. 2:11-14
4. Legalism is susceptible to promoting hypocrisy.   d. Gal. 5:15
5. Legalism threatens the truth of the gospel.   e. Gal. 2:5
6. Legalism is highly contagious within a church.   f. Gal. 4:15

(Answers: 1d, 2f, 3a, 4c, 5e, 6b)

A Personal Testimony (Gal. 1:11-24)

After exposing how the Galatians Christians had drifted away from the gospel of Christ, Paul went on to validate the message he had preached to them years earlier. He certified the authority of his message by sharing his testimony regarding how the gospel message had come to him. Eager to set the record straight for anyone who may have doubted him, he asserted that no human being had given him instruction on the gospel he preached. Paul hadn't sat at the feet of one of the apostles dutifully taking notes on the message so he could share it just as they had given it to him. Neither had he memorized the message from a written document that someone had given him so he could deliver it properly.

Paul asserted that he didn't receive the message of the gospel through human instruction at all. The Lord had revealed it to him (1:12). Paul traced the events in his life that led up to the moment when Christ revealed Himself to him. In his testimony Paul described the life he lived before he encountered Jesus (1:13-14). He brought up his misplaced zeal for God that made him a religious activist bent on getting rid of Christians. He also added some facts about his pedigree that had him at the top of the heap in the Jewish world. His pedigree coupled with his zeal promised him a place of honor among his people for his work as a persecutor of Christians.

Christ turned Paul's world upside down. After meeting Jesus, Paul stopped persecuting Christians and started proclaiming the gospel. Gentiles as well as Jews came to Christ because of Paul's preaching ministry. Paul's testimony of God's grace in Christ had a radical effect on the lives of people who heard the message he proclaimed.

All who have received Christ have a story to share about spiritual transformation.

Not everyone who receives Christ will become a vocational missionary, but all who have received Christ have a story to share about spiritual transformation. It's a story about an encounter with Christ that has made an eternal difference in our lives. It's a story others need to hear.

A CLOSER LOOK

God's Grace and God's Glory

God's glory has to do with His reputation. In the Old Testament, God's glory signified the heaviness of His presence or the weightiness of His influence in His world. In the New Testament, His glory was connected with the praise due Him because of His grace. God's grace to us refers to His blessings to us even though we don't deserve them. Of course, the supreme expression of His grace comes our way through Jesus Christ. Our Lord's birth, life, death, and resurrection will always be the Father's most gracious blessing to us. When we receive God's gift of salvation through Christ, we glorify Him. Others glorify Him as well when they see the eternal change He has made in us.

As Paul continued to share his testimony, he mentioned meeting Peter (1:18-19). This was three years after meeting Christ on the Damascus road. When Paul met Peter in Jerusalem, he visited with him and James for only 15 days. He didn't go to Jerusalem to learn the gospel from Peter. Neither Peter nor James had coached Paul on what to say about the good news of Christ.

From Jerusalem, Paul returned directly to the mission field, preaching the gospel everywhere he went. The good news of Christ he preached had a

tremendous effect on the people who heard it. Lives everywhere were being changed for eternity. Back in Jerusalem, the Christians glorified God for the way He had transformed Paul's life and used him as a messenger of God's grace in Christ (1:23-24).

Paul's testimony provides a helpful way for believers today to share Christ. By describing our lives before we met Christ, explaining how we received Him, and

Above: The eastern gate of Damascus looking from the inside to out. Paul met Christ on the road to Damascus, was baptized there, and began his preaching ministry there (Acts 9:18-20; Gal. 1:17).

talking about the difference He's made in us since He saved us, our testimony can have a powerful effect on others. We never know what will happen as we share our story of God's grace to us in Christ.

In the introduction to Paul's letter, we gain insight into God's grace. Each of us who know God through Christ can point to a number of expressions of His grace in our lives. However, the central and most glorious expression of His grace is what He has done for us in Jesus Christ. When we receive salvation through Christ and grow to become mature disciples, we provide the best demonstration of His grace. By following Him faithfully, we can make an eternal difference in the lives of individuals who need to know Christ for themselves. For that reason, we need to express His grace to us in Christ and encourage other believers to remain faithful to Him alone.

For Your Consideration

1. Why did Paul stress that he did not receive the gospel from a human source?

2. Where did Paul go after he received Christ?

3. Who was the last person with whom you shared your testimony?

Left: View of the Taurus Mountain Range, which was on the southeastern border between Galatia and Cilicia.

My Testimony According to Grace

In Paul's autobiographical description of his life before Christ (1:13-24), he provided a model for sharing a testimony about the impact of grace on a person's life. Use the outline below to develop your own testimony about how God's grace has changed your life.

1. My life before grace

2. How I found grace

3. My life after grace

Chapter 2
Galatians 2:1-21

NO OTHER WAY

Sandy could hardly wait to spend her first night in her new apartment. Her bedroom at home had become too cramped, and her parents had begun to get on her nerves. Now that she had a new job, she didn't need to live at home anymore anyway. And besides, all of her friends had moved into places of their own. The time had come for her to take the same step.

Getting ready to move out took priority for her. In fact, it became something like an obsession. She imaged where she would hang her pictures, how she could stock her kitchen, and which pieces of furniture to purchase so she could get off to a good start. When the day finally arrived to move, she whispered a glad good-bye to her parents' careful watch over her. She loved them both, but she had changed. She needed to be on her own.

After only a couple of weeks in her new apartment, however, she started to miss home, her parents, and their supervision in her life. Life under their roof had given her a sense of security. She began to wish that she could return to the security of her bedroom at home.

The Galatians seemed bent on abandoning their freedom in Christ and returning to a works-based religion. Paul reminded them that faith in Christ alone had set them free. For that reason they needed to guard against the urge to return to spiritual slavery under the Law.

Recognizing Grace (Gal. 2:1-10)

As Paul validated the authority of the gospel he preached, he mentioned two trips to Jerusalem in his letter to the Galatians. He pointed out that he met some of the apostles on his first visit to Jerusalem (1:11-21). He went on to say that he made a return trip to Jerusalem 14 years later. Paul ran into open conflict on the return visit because of the gospel he preached to the Gentiles.

Paul said that he returned to Jerusalem only after God revealed to him that he needed to make the trip (2:2). The apostle's second trip could have been his visit to deliver much-needed resources to the Christians there who suffered because of the severe famine at that time (Acts 11:27-30). Or it could have been his visit to attend an important meeting of church leaders. They gathered to discuss the relationship between Gentile and Jewish Christians (Acts 15:1-21). Regardless of which trip he had in mind, Paul asserted that he went to Jerusalem a second time because God led him to return. The apostles in Jerusalem had not invited him.

Titus, a Gentile Christian, joined Paul on his second trip to Jerusalem. Paul brought him along in order to drive home an important point. Titus had been saved by faith alone. For that reason Paul didn't instruct him to be circumcised (2:3). Gentiles didn't have to keep Jewish laws in order to become Christians.

Paul's unbending position regarding Titus helps us see the value of taking a stand for doctrinal truth. When we hear doctrinal errors being promoted as truths, we may prefer to remain silent. Our preference for silence may be due to the fact that we don't like to confront other Christians. But remaining silent will render a worse outcome. New believers may stumble spiritually, and lost people may never come to Christ. Therefore, let us stand firm for vital Christian doctrines.

Let us stand firm for vital Christian doctrines.

Paul got into trouble because of his stand. He had made an assortment of enemies throughout his missionary work. His adversaries insisted that faith alone couldn't save anyone. For them, salvation came from keeping the rules and regulations set forth in the Old Testament. They favored legalistic observance of religious rules and scorned the truth about spiritual freedom in Christ. Because they stood rigidly against salvation by faith alone and favored observing the rigid laws of Judaism, they became known as Judaizers.

Apparently a team of Judaizers had secretly slipped into a meeting and listened as Paul discussed the gospel with other church leaders in Jerusalem (2:4). Before long, they disrupted the gathering by trying to refute Paul. Of course, their attempt failed because Paul refused to bend (2:5). He treasured freedom in Christ too much to back down from the truth of the gospel. The Galatian Christians benefited from the stand Paul took. They got to hear the gospel of salvation by simple faith alone (2:5).

Along with giving him victory over his enemies, Paul's visit to Jerusalem had other positive results. The leaders of the church in Jerusalem—Peter, James, and John—confirmed the truth of the gospel Paul proclaimed. They also affirmed his ministry to the Gentiles in the same way they encouraged Peter's missionary work with Jewish people (2:7-10).

The affirmation given to Paul teaches us an important lesson. We can expect tremendous results when we work together as a body of believers in sharing the gospel of Christ. God works through His church when we unify ourselves under the common purpose of sharing Christ with all people everywhere. A unified church is a powerful force in God's hands.

A unified church is a powerful force in God's hands.

For Your Consideration

1. Along with Titus, who went with Paul on his return trip to Jerusalem?

2. How can diluting doctrinal truth lead to spiritual enslavement?

3. Who in your life needs you to explain that salvation comes by simple faith in Christ alone?

Word Search on Galatians 2:6-10

				U							
1				**U**							
	2			**N**							
		3		**I**							
	4			**T**							
		5		**E**							
	6			**D**							

1. Description of Paul's relationship to the gospel (v. 7)
2. One of the pillars of the church of Jerusalem (v. 9)
3. The hand of fellowship extended to Paul and Barnabas (v. 9)
4. What was added to Paul's gospel during his visit to Jerusalem (v. 6)
5. The apostle through whom God was at work among the circumcised (v. 8)
6. Paul's opinion of men who are recognized as important (v. 6)

Answers: 1. Entrusted; 2. John; 3. Right; 4. Nothing; 5. Peter; 6. No difference

Rejecting Hypocrisy (Gal. 2:11-14)

Paul's testimony has something to say about being good role models. Christians who serve together can make a decisive difference in kingdom work with the example they set. The story of Paul's relationship with Peter, James, and John in Jerusalem gives us an excellent illustration of cooperation in fulfilling the Great Commission. By talking and praying together, discerning the key doctrinal issues at hand, celebrating accomplishments, and dividing up the work yet to be done, we can set a fine pattern for other Christians. As we take seriously the Great Commission assignment today, we can look to the first-century apostles as inspiring models. In turn, we can be good role models ourselves as we work together with other believers.

When we do something that contradicts the gospel, our behavior sets an example for other believers as well, albeit a bad example. In particular, modeling hypocrisy can have an appalling effect on a vulnerable Christian. Wise

Christians know the damaging effects of hypocritical behavior on younger believers and will do everything possible to avoid it.

Spiritual Hypocrisy

Being a hypocrite involves pretending. In the Old Testament the Hebrew word translated **hypocrite** carried the notion of pollution or corruption. In the New Testament the Greek word for *hypocrite* described actors who played a role, pretending to be someone other than themselves. The word came to denote a pretentious or insincere person. In Matthew 23, Jesus used the word to show His disgust with the behavior of religious leaders. Paul warned Christians against hypocrisy, and so did Peter (1 Tim 4:21; 1 Pet. 2:1). They encouraged believers to be sincere in their relationship with God and one another.

That's why Paul confronted Peter at the church in Antioch (2:11). Peter's hypocrisy needed to be exposed because of the negative example he was setting for other Christians. Paul's commitment to the good news of Christ and his love for believers wouldn't allow him to sit idly by while Peter behaved like a hypocrite.

The church in Antioch had a special place in Paul's heart. Early in his ministry Paul accepted Barnabas's invitation to join him in Antioch to work with the believers there. Together they led the congregation to grow in Christ (Acts 11:19-26). In due time the church at Antioch sent Paul and Barnabas on their first missionary journey (Acts 13:1-3). The Antioch church was a diverse congregation. Some of the Christians there came from Gentile backgrounds while others had deep roots in Judaism. Apparently Paul and Barnabas had worked diligently with the church there to remove the religious and cultural barriers in their relationships with one another.

Paul recounted the facts related to Peter's visit to Antioch. On his visit, Peter made every effort at first to show Gentile Christians how he loved them as much as he loved the Jewish believers. He demonstrated his

love by eating with Gentile believers (Gal. 2:12a). In those days Jews detested Gentiles. They considered Gentiles to be unclean. Consequently, having a meal with them would have been out of the question. When Peter, a Jewish believer, opened his arms to Gentile Christians in Antioch, he sent a clear message of love and acceptance in the Lord. By taking meals with Gentile Christians, Peter also validated the truth that salvation by faith in Christ turns believers into spiritual siblings.

Peter changed his behavior radically, however, when a group of Judaizers showed up at the church in Antioch. In their presence Peter treated Gentile Christians like second-class citizens. Instead of eating with them, he turned his nose up at them so he could win the favor of the Judaizers (2:12b). Before long, other Jewish Christians followed his example. Even Barnabas joined him in his hypocrisy (2:13).

Legalism had lured Peter and Barnabas into hypocrisy. Legalism made religious snobbery acceptable to them. They could enjoy the safety of an elite group that included only certain people who kept a set of religious rules. Of course, returning to legalism made Peter feel more comfortable, certain, and secure.

The example Peter set with his hypocrisy contradicted the gospel Peter himself proclaimed. He preached freedom in Christ, but he acted like legalism mattered more. Left unchallenged, Peter's actions would have devastated the church. Paul had no choice but to rebuke him in front of the entire congregation. What Peter had done needed to be exposed and rebuked. It threatened the sweet but fragile fellowship among the believers, and it contradicted the gospel. For Paul, the good news of Christ could not be compromised because of Peter's hypocrisy.

Left: St Peter's Church at Antioch. The church was built into the side of a cliff by late first-century Christians, and named after Peter from its beginning. The inside is 1st century. The present facade was added by 11th-century Christians

For Your Consideration

1. Why did Paul confront Peter in Antioch?

2. How can a preference for keeping religious rules lure a Christian into hypocrisy today?

3. What personal changes do you need to make in order to be a better example of freedom in Christ?

Hypocrisy

How susceptible are you to the lure of hypocrisy in your life? Respond to the statements below with T if it is true about you and F if it does not describe you.

____ I worry a great deal about what people think about me.

____ My reputation is more important than anything else.

____ Taking a stand on controversial issues is never worth it.

____ It is just too stressful to confront people with the truth, and I avoid doing it.

____ People can't be expected to practice everything they believe.

____ I have friends at church and friends at work, but I don't want them to meet each other.

Made Righteous by Faith Alone (Gal. 2:15-21)

After sharing his testimony, Paul launched into a pointed argument about grace. He turned his attention to two supreme expressions of God's grace to sinners. He insisted that salvation could only come by faith (2:15-18) and that Christ alone could give new life (2:19-21).

Written to believers in the 1st century, Paul's argument still resonates with believers in the 21st century. With Paul we insist that salvation by faith alone expresses God's grace to sinners. Although the differences between Jews and Gentiles in Paul's day don't frequently come up in our interactions with one another today, we still have distinctions that tend to separate us. In our various cultural, social, economic, or racial groups, we can see ourselves as better than others. Left to ourselves, we keep on trying to separate ourselves from others.

Like people of Paul's day and every generation after him, we find ourselves trying to have a relationship with God on our own terms. We attempt to keep certain rules, observe selected rituals, or perform prescribed duties. But the gospel of Jesus Christ shatters our notions about earning God's favor by asserting that all people everywhere suffer from the same problem—all of us are sinners. For that reason, we cannot earn a relationship with God, no matter how hard we try.

Left: Dating from the first century B.C., a terra cotta vessel in the form of a comic actor impersonating a slave seated on an altar. The Greek word for *hypocrite* described an actor who played a role (Gal. 2:13).

ILLUSTRATOR PHOTO/ DAVID ROGERS/ BRITISH MUSEUM/ LONDON

We find ourselves trying to have a relationship with God on our own terms.

Because of our sinfulness, we stand before God like convicted criminals facing a judge for sentencing. Our sins have condemned us, and we deserve the sentence of death. Nothing we can do will erase our sins. No matter how much we work or how many rules we try to keep, we can't take away our sins or the penalty to be paid for them.

In such a dismal courtroom setting, imagine the judge doing something absolutely inconceivable. Instead of condemning us to die, picture the judge pardoning us and letting us go free. Ponder the shock on our faces and the joy in our hearts as the bailiff removes the shackles that bind our hands and feet. Such a magnificent and glorious scene of freedom gives us a glimpse into what God in His grace has done to justify us.

When the Lord saved us, He pardoned us even though our sins condemned us to death. God, in His grace, gave His Son to pay the penalty for our sin so we could be forgiven and freed from sin's penalty and power. We receive God's gracious pardon when we welcome Christ into our lives by simple faith.

Growing Christians cannot give in to the notion that we are able to earn God's favor on our own. Trying something so futile can be described as nothing less than an awful sin against God (2:18). Christ alone gives us spiritual liberty and new life. Our sins have been nailed to His cross. We have died to our old attempt to earn peace with God. Now we live to serve Him because He saved us when we placed our faith in Him.

Having been saved by faith, we also affirm with Paul that Christ lives in us. Christ supplies strength for daily living to those who trust Him (2:20). He will give us what we need each day so we can serve Him. The reality of Christ's love for us by giving Himself for us prompts us to express our love for Him by living for Him.

If we could be made right on our own, then Jesus didn't need to die for us on the cross.

Christ alone makes us righteous. If we could be made right on our own, then Jesus didn't need to die for us on the cross. Only He can give us a right standing with God. It's not possible by our attempts to earn God's favor. It's only possible by trusting Christ.

A CLOSER LOOK

Being Righteous

In our day, being **righteous** generally means possessing certain virtues. The biblical meaning, however, involves having a relationship. A righteous person has a growing relationship with God. We become righteous in our walk with God by living according to the terms of the relationship. For legalists, the terms can only be fulfilled by tedious attention to a prescribed set of tenets or regulations. By contrast, Christians know that God makes us righteous the moment we receive His gift of salvation through simple faith in Jesus Christ.

This portion of Paul's letter reminds us of the sole source of our security. When we received Christ, we gave up on working to win God's favor. Instead, we embraced new life in Christ as a gift of God's grace. We received His gift by simple faith.

Along the way, however, our need for spiritual security may lead us to elbow out a walk of faith and exchange it for legalism. Before long, we can lose sight of faith and see nothing but a religious checklist. Although we say with our words that we live by faith in Christ, we may say with our lives that we prefer legalism over freedom.

Although we say with our words that we live by faith in Christ, we may say with our lives that we prefer legalism over freedom.

Paul reminded us that faith in Christ alone renders the contentment we need in our walk with Him. No other way exists for anyone to have a healthy, growing relationship with the Lord. Our search for security always ends in trusting Christ, the ultimate expression of His grace to us.

For Your Consideration

1. According to Paul, what do we set aside if we think we can earn our salvation?

2. What do we mean when we say that we have been crucified with Christ?

3. How will you demonstrate in your relationships at work or at home that Christ lives in you?

Chapter 3
Galatians 3:1-25

BIBLE TRUTH

Grace has always been the focus of God's salvation provision.

LIFE GOAL

To help you understand that faith in Christ is the only means of salvation and put your faith in Him

W alking together in the park one day, Kaci and her grandfather had a conversation about his family. Keenly interested for a moment in her great-grandparents, Kaci asked him to tell her his mother's name.

"Grace."

"Wow, that's a pretty name."

"And she lived up to it," Grandpa said in a reflective sort of way.

"What do you mean?"

Grandpa proceeded to tell Kaci why he thought his mother was worthy of the name "Grace." He described her loving ways directed toward him and his two sisters. He told Kaci the story about the day he accidentally shattered the neighbor's window. He threw a rock that had gotten off course. Knowing that he would get into big trouble, he went straight home to tell her what he had done.

She walked with him to the neighbor's house and stood nearby as he made his confession to the home owner. Then she arranged to pay the cost of repairing the window.

"I didn't deserve my mom's kind and loving ways. That's why her name fit her so well."

In this portion of Paul's letter to the Christians at Galatia, Paul paints the gift of salvation that we receive by faith in the rich colors of God's grace. By saving us through Christ, He gave us what we didn't deserve. What Paul has written helps us to grow more confident in God's grace expressed supremely in Jesus Christ.

Confirmed by Experience (Gal. 3:1-5)

Paul made no attempt to hide his frustration with the Galatian Christians. They couldn't deny that the message of Christ's death on the cross had made an indelible mark on them. They could never erase from their memories the gripping portrayal of His crucifixion for their salvation.

Now they behaved as if they had all but completely forgotten what Christ had done for them. Only one reason could be given for such frustrating behavior. Someone had come into their fellowship and hypnotized them, so to speak, deceiving them into thinking that faith in Christ alone couldn't have saved them. The unnamed malicious enemy of the gospel had won their trust and led them to dismiss the liberating gospel and to embrace religious legalism.

As Paul tried to break the spell of legalism that had been cast over them, he brought up the law (3:2). In Paul's day the law referred primarily to the Ten Commandments, but it also included other Old Testament commandments. The Jewish leaders studied meticulously to determine what a person had to do in order to abide by the law. They came to believe that being right with God meant doing what the law required. Consequently, a relationship with God required a person to work diligently at keeping the law as the Jewish leaders interpreted it. Strict observance of the law as the only way to have a relationship with God became known as legalism.

Salvation by faith in Jesus Christ stands in direct opposition to legalism. That's why Paul grieved over the step backward into spiritual slavery the Galatian Christians had taken. Having gotten off to a good start by faith in Christ, they seemed to behave as if growing toward spiritual maturity required keeping the law.

Salvation by faith in Jesus Christ stands in direct opposition to legalism.

To challenge their shift toward legalism, Paul asked them a probing question (3:2). If they answered the question correctly, they would demonstrate for themselves how foolish they had been. They would have no choice but to agree with him that trying to keep the law wouldn't win God's favor.

The question in verse 2 relates to the presence of the Holy Spirit in their lives. Paul wanted to know how the Holy Spirit had come to dwell within them. If they had received the Holy Spirit by practicing legalism, then they should continue to devote themselves to keeping the law. However, if they had received the Holy Spirit by placing their faith in Christ, they should stay on the path of freedom in Him. Drawing attention to the work of the Holy Spirit in their lives, Paul encouraged them to reflect for a moment. He asked them to recollect some key experiences that may have faded from their memories in their drift toward legalism. He asked them to recall how they had served the Lord with all their hearts and suffered for Him apparently without complaint. Also, he wanted them to remember how God performed miracles among them (3:5). Remembering these experiences could enable the Galatian Christians to recall that the Holy Spirit had come to dwell in them when they received Christ by simple faith.

Recalling our experience of salvation can help us in our walk with Christ today. The moment we received Christ, the Holy Spirit came to dwell within us. The Holy Spirit opened our minds so we could begin to grasp the truths of God's Word, warmed our hearts so we could enjoy a personal relationship with Him, and directed our actions so we could please Him. And it all happened the moment we trusted Christ to save us. The presence of the Holy Spirit in our lives didn't result from working hard to keep a set of religious rules. He came to dwell in us when Jesus saved us. The indwelling of the Holy Spirit points to the reality of salvation by grace through faith.

For Your Consideration

1. Why was Paul frustrated with the Galatians and how did he reflect his frustration in these verses?

2. How does a person receive the Holy Spirit?

3. How does the indwelling of the Holy Spirit point to the reality of salvation by grace?

Emphasized in the Old Testament (Gal. 3:6-18)

To affirm the essential role of faith in salvation, Paul pointed the Galatians to the Old Testament. He called their attention to Abraham. Faith took center stage in Abraham's life. Paul recounted Genesis 15:6 to prove the centrality of faith in Abraham's relationship with God. Abraham didn't walk with God because he had earned that privilege by keeping religious rules. Rather, the door for a relationship with God opened when Abraham placed his trust in Him. Abraham's faith alone had made him right with God.

Paul went on to underscore the promise God made to Abraham as a result of his faith. God promised to bless Abraham and his descendents (Gen. 12:3). Paul highlighted the promise to show the Galatian Christians how Abraham's relationship with God started. It didn't begin with Abraham's attempting to keep enough rules so he could earn God's favor. Rather, it began with God's promising Abraham that He would bless all people everywhere. Abraham's faith had made him righteous in God's eyes (Gal. 3:6). Likewise, the Galatian believers could rest assured that their faith in Christ had made them right with God too (3:9).

Paul next called attention to the law and the curse associated with it. In verse 10 Paul quoted Deuteronomy 27:26. He asserted that people who couldn't keep God's law found themselves under the curse of His judgment. Curiously, anyone who hung on a tree would be accursed as well (Deut. 21:23). When Jesus died on the cross, He bore our curse so we could receive the blessing God promised Abraham (Gal. 3:13-14). Therefore, everyone everywhere can receive the same blessing of a relationship with God by placing their trust in Christ. Because Jesus died for everyone, Gentiles as well as Jews can receive His gift of salvation.

Two certainties regarding our walk with God come into view from Paul's explanation of the law. First, we cannot grow in our relationship with God by devoting ourselves to legalism. We deceive ourselves if we think that legalism is the pathway to spiritual maturity. If we disobey even one of God's commandments, we have broken His entire law. Breaking His law leaves a person accursed and under God's judgment (3:13). Therefore, growing in godliness by practicing legalism simply can't be done.

Growing in godliness by practicing legalism simply can't be done.

Second, God can be trusted to keep His promises. God promised Abraham that through him all people would be blessed. On the cross God kept the promise He made to Abraham. That's why we can rest assured that Jesus fulfilled God's intention to bless the nations in keeping with His promise to Abraham (3:15-16).

A CLOSER LOOK

The Value of a Covenant

Paul mentioned God's covenant with Abraham twice in this portion of Galatians (3:15,17). In the Old Testament, a **covenant** served as a binding agreement between two parties. Covenants could be made between two people or parties. For instance, David and Jonathan made an official pact to confirm their friendship (1 Sam. 18:3). Also, God took the initiative to make covenants with His people. In His covenant with Abraham, He made a promise. He promised to bless Abraham and his descendents and to work through them to bless everyone in the world. Abraham entered into the covenant with God by placing his trust in Him (Gen. 15).

If we believe that we grow in our walk with God by practicing legalism, then we will generally prefer to talk about the law. We will tend to focus primarily on what happened at Mount Sinai when God gave His law to His people (Ex. 20). If we settle there, however, we do ourselves an injustice. Let's give attention first to God's encounter with Abraham. Reading the account of Abraham's call in Genesis 12 takes us back 430 years before Mount Sinai. That's when Abraham placed his faith in God. In that moment God considered him to be righteous and nurtured a relationship with him. For that reason we insist with Paul that God's relationship with us is based on a promise He fulfilled in Jesus Christ. Because of the promise God kept in Christ, we can enjoy the inheritance He promised Abraham (Gal. 3:18).

For Your Consideration

1. How did Abraham gain favor with God?

Above: Plain of Raha with the peaks of Jebel Musa, traditional Mount Sinai, in the background. God revealed His law to Moses on Mount Sinai.

2. Who are the true children of Abraham?

3. What does God's promise to Abraham say about His grace toward His people today?

Scripture Match

Match the verse in Galatians 3 on the right with the Old Testament reference on the left. (Note: a verse can have more than one answer)

1. Verse 6
2. Verse 8
3. Verse 10
4. Verse 11
5. Verse 12
6. Verse 13
7. Verse 16

a. Habakkuk 2:4
b. Genesis 13:15
c. Genesis 12:3
d. Genesis 24:7
e. Genesis 15:16
f. Genesis 12:7
g. Deuteronomy 21:23
h. Deuteronomy 27:26
i. Genesis 17:8
j. Leviticus 18:5

Answers: 1e, 2c, 3h, 4a, 5j, 6g, 7/bibd

Affirmed by the Law's Intent (Gal. 3:19-25)

Paul asserted that what happened at Mount Sinai mattered but not in the way the Galatian Christians had been led to believe. He clarified the intent of the law. God gave the law to His people on Mount Sinai for one important reason. He provided them with the standard that He would use in judging them. The standard of the law would allow them to see their transgressions clearly. Seeing their actions in light of the law, the hard fact that they had sinned against God would become indisputable.

A CLOSER LOOK

What Is a Transgression?

In Galatians 3:19, Paul used the word "transgressions" to describe sins. In both the Hebrew and Greek languages, God's Word describes sin in a number of different ways. For instance, it's described as missing the mark, violating God's righteous nature, rebelling against God, and breaking covenant with God. The word **transgression** offers a unique description of sin because its relationship to the law. The word *transgression* literally means "to step across a line." Stepping across a property line or stepping out of bounds on a basketball court helps us get a clear picture of what it means to transgress. Accordingly, when we step across the line regarding God's law, we commit a transgression.

The law leaves us with a clear understanding that we have sinned against God. Without the law we would set our own subjective standard for living, and it would be wrong. Our self-made subjective standard allows us to deceive ourselves into excusing our sinful behavior. It leads us to determine what's right and wrong based on our own sin-infested inclinations.

Bob went to the doctor for his yearly checkup, but he didn't really consider the visit necessary. As he sat in the waiting room, he felt absolutely fine. His self-diagnosis made him toy with the notion that he should cancel his appointment and go home. Before he could make a decision, however, the nurse called his name and escorted him to the examination room. On his way he had to stand on the scale to be weighed. Much to his surprise, he discovered that he had gained some weight. Later the doctor informed Bob that his blood test showed an unusually high bad cholesterol count. He also shared with Bob that his blood pressure seemed to be extremely high.

As it turned out, Bob had some serious health problems even though he felt fine. The standards established by medical science to measure physical health had proven to Bob that he was not well. They also convinced him that he needed his doctor's help after all.

The law provides God's standard for measuring our spiritual health. It shows that we have some serious spiritual problems and that we need help if we intend to remedy them. In other words, the law convinces us that we need Christ. We can never expect to get well spiritually on our own, no matter what we do or how hard we try. The help we need can come only from Jesus Christ.

We can never expect to get well spiritually on our own, no matter what we do or how hard we try.

Christians who turn away from simple faith in Christ to embrace legalism ignore an important fact of spiritual life. If practicing legalism could save someone, then God's promise to Abraham wouldn't have been necessary (3:21). The same truth can be expressed in another way. If keeping the law can produce spiritual vitality in our lives, then we wouldn't need God's gracious gift of salvation through Christ. We could be right with God on our own by keeping the law.

But trying to do what the law requires can never give us spiritual freedom or spiritual vitality. Quite the contrary, the law condemns us. God has declared in His Word the truth about our sin and its consequences. Our sin made us stand condemned before God, and the law locked us away in a spiritual prison. When Christ came, He tore down the prison bars for us when we placed our faith in Him (3:23).

According to Paul, the law has also served as a guardian (3:24-25). The Galatian Christians understood the custom among aristocratic parents to enlist a guardian to supervise their child's activities. Guardians could be ruthless in their mistreatment of children in their care. At the hand of the heartless guardian, children faced misery, and every day the harsh treatment would only get worse. When children finally reached the legal age of adulthood, they could be set free from the guardian's supervision.

Against the backdrop of the law as a guardian, consider what Christ has done for us. When He came into our lives by faith,

He liberated us from the spiritual torment we endured because of the law. At the same time, He gave us the blessing of an intimate relationship with Him.

Paul's description of the law as a guardian challenges us to reflect on God's grace to us through Jesus Christ. Reflect for a moment on the benefits of His grace. When we received Christ by faith, we experienced the indwelling of His Spirit. Furthermore, we received the blessing He promised Abraham generations ago. Equally important, we were set free from the condemnation of the law and all of the torment that went along with it. When we reflect on these precious benefits of His grace, our hearts overflow with gratitude to Him and with resolve to avoid legalism in our walk with Him.

Left: Hammurabi's code. Seven feet high in black basalt, this stela is inscribed with a collection of laws from the reign of king Hammurabi, ruler of Babylon from 1792 to 1750 B.C. Extrabiblical laws reflected the authority of earthly kings. God's law reflects His greater authority, His unchanging standards, and our need for grace.

For Your Consideration

1. Why did God give the law?

2. How is trying to be right with God through keeping the law like being in prison?

3. Which benefit of God's grace in Christ do you need to thank Him for today?

Confidence in Grace

1:3	Grace comes from God the Father and our Lord Jesus Christ.
1:6	The gospel message is a declaration of grace.
1:15	God's call to salvation is an act of His grace.
2:9	Our ministry effectiveness comes from God and His grace.
2:21	Because of grace, believers are made righteous in God's sight.
5:4	Seeking salvation by works is to renounce salvation by grace.
6:18	Grace is God's favor toward sinful people .

The word *grace* appears seven times in Galatians and describes God's undeserved favor and kindness in offering sinful people salvation and righteousness apart from their works. The Galatians had lost their confidence in grace's ability to secure their condition before God.

Why do believers today sometimes lose confidence in God's grace?

What are some signs that a person is confident in God's grace?

What effects should grace have on our emotional and spiritual lives?

Chapter 4
Galatians 3:26–4:7

BLE TRUTH

nly through God's
ace can people from
fferent backgrounds
xperience genuine
ity.

FE GOAL

 help you
derstand that
ith in Christ is
e only means of
lvation and put
ur faith in Him

THE COMMUNITY OF GRACE

Claude and Martha wanted their children and grandchildren to join them for a family portrait. For them, their 50th wedding anniversary wouldn't be complete without it. A picture of the family that resulted from five decades of marriage would be the best gift they could ever receive.

The people who sat for the picture represented a huge diversity of thoughts, opinions, and attitudes. Claude and Martha's three children expressed extremely different political views, which sometimes made family gatherings a little stressful. Their spouses added to the tension when they chimed in with their own opinions.

The 10 grandchildren made the family even more diverse. Each grandchild represented a different personality and set of life experiences. However, when they got together, they enjoyed talking with one another about what they had in common. Being members of Claude and Martha's family obviously was important to them.

When everyone sat for the picture, they found a place around Claude and Martha, who sat in the middle. They stood close to one another and smiled for the camera. The picture that resulted became the happy couple's favorite treasure. It was a snapshot of their family composed of diverse people unified by the people in the middle of the picture.

Being a Christian means being a member of God's family. Although each of us may be different from other believers in many ways, our unity comes from our common devotion to Christ. Because of God's grace in Christ, we portray authentic unity as members of God's family.

The Means of Unity (Gal. 3:26)

Earlier in Galatians 3, Paul explained the connection between God's promise to Abraham and our life in Christ. He also devoted attention to clarifying the purpose of the law. Paul then made a profound declaration. He declared that the Galatian Christians were God's children because they had placed their faith in Christ (3:26).

Notice three compelling features of Paul's declaration. First, Paul used the word *you* in his appeal to the Galatian believers. Paul, a seasoned Old Testament scholar, had laid out plenty of historical facts to support the gospel of faith he proclaimed. With this declaration, however, Paul got extremely personal with his Christian friends. He wanted them to apply the truth about Christ to their lives. For that reason he didn't use "them" or "us" in his appeal to them. Instead, Paul used "you" as he appealed to the Galatian believers. He gave the impression that he was looking directly into their eyes as he pressed them to see themselves as God's children because they had received Christ by faith.

Second, Paul used the word *all* in his declaration. By using this word, he set aside ethnic and cultural differences within the churches. The word *all* resolved the tensions between Jewish and Gentile believers. Both groups could rest assured that they had the same standing before God.

Third, Paul used the word *faith* in his declaration. He declared that faith in Christ had made the Galatians members of God's family. Earlier, Paul confirmed that Jesus was God's Son (1:15-16; 2:20). Now Paul assured the Galatians that they could consider themselves sons—or children—of God. Of course, God's Son reigned supreme in His family. Because of His sacrifice, however, they became God's children when they gave their lives to Him by faith.

The three compelling features of Paul's declaration continue to give us assurance. We join God's family when we receive His gift of salvation. All believers everywhere become members of God's family in the same way. Our trust in Him unites us as a family of believers who share a common devotion to serve Him.

All believers everywhere become members of God's family in the same way.

Our spiritual unity helps us overcome the barriers that ethnic, racial, or cultural differences tend to construct. Like the Galatian Christians who could set their cultural differences aside in their common devotion to Christ, we can thank Him for removing the barriers that separate us from other believers. Faith in Jesus Christ makes all Christians members of God's family. We know one another as brothers and sisters in Christ.

For Your Consideration

1. What had the Galatian Christians done that qualified them to be God's children?

2. What are some potential barriers to the unity of believers today?

Crossword Puzzle on Galatians 3:26

"*For you are all sons of God through faith in Christ Jesus.*"

ACROSS

2. The word that transcends differences between believers in Christ
3. The only means of salvation
4. The family status of everyone who places their trust in Christ
5. Paul's personal form of address to the Galatians

DOWN

1. The ultimate source of all unity among believers

Answers: Across: 2. ALL; 3. FAITH, 4. SONS OF GOD; 5. YOU; Down: 1. CHRIST JESUS

The Expression of Unity (Gal. 3:27)

Regardless of our status in society, God welcomes us into His family when we receive Christ. In His family He grants us spiritual kinship with other believers. Even though we come into His family from different cultures and backgrounds, we have something in common that transcends anything that makes us different from one another.

According to Paul, we express our spiritual unity as believers in a way that genuinely honors Christ. As members of God's family, baptism expresses our linkage with Him as our Heavenly Father and with one another as spiritual siblings (3:27). In baptism we display the grace of God who clothed us with new life and spiritual freedom in Christ. Also, we portray our relationship with our brothers and sisters in Christ who have been baptized after receiving God's gift of salvation through Christ.

A CLOSER LOOK

Putting on Christ

The picture of taking off and putting on clothes (Gal. 3:27) served Paul well as he instructed believers about their relationship with Christ. For example, he used the picture to help Christians see the richly symbolic connection between being baptized and living for Jesus (Rom. 6–8). He also incorporated the picture when he encouraged Christians to give up their pagan habits and practices and to embrace character traits that would reflect their walk with Jesus (Rom. 13:11-14). As he urged Christians to be prepared for the ongoing battles in spiritual warfare, he used the picture of clothing again. He insisted that believers should put on the whole armor of God (Eph. 6:11-14).

The opponents of the gospel in Paul's day wanted Christians to express their salvation through circumcision. They insisted that believers needed to be circumcised to show that they had given themselves to God. For them, circumcision proved that Christians had surrendered themselves to keeping the law.

By being circumcised, however, believers would also express their intention to embrace other facets of Judaism. Circumcision in this context was a bad mistake in an erroneous attempt to earn favor with God by keeping the law. That's why Paul opposed it so vigorously. Being circumcised would turn out to be nothing more than the first step in a forced march to the spiritual prison constructed by legalism.

Above: The Jordan River at Bethany-Beyond-the-Jordan. John the Baptist baptized Jesus in the Jordan River at Bethany (John 1:28).

Paul's perspective on baptism continues to resonate with believers today. Baptism is a reflection of our devotion in Christ and an authentic expression of our unity with other Christians. Through baptism new Christians identify with both Christ and other believers. For that reason baptism serves believers well as the symbol of our entry into God's family.

Baptism is a reflection of our devotion in Christ and an authentic expression of our unity with other Christians.

We must not allow baptism to be viewed as a second-class feature in our worship. The ordinance of baptism should be seen as an important action in worship through which new believers identify themselves with Christ and others who make up God's family. The identifying mark of baptism connects us with one another in Christ. Thus, our worship services should reflect that biblical reality.

Carlos serves as a pastor and takes baptism seriously. So does his church. Prior to worship services in which he baptizes new believers, he reminds the new converts what baptism means. He tells them about Christians who suffer persecution because they have given themselves to Jesus. Then he points out to new believers that baptism demonstrates their kinship with these persecuted Christians. He encourages them to take their identity seriously in keeping with the example set by their spiritual siblings in God's family.

For Your Consideration

1. How did the Galatian Christians demonstrate that they had given themselves to Christ?

2. Why does baptism serve so well as a mark of identity for Christians?

3. Who in your church needs your encouragement regarding his or her place in God's family?

The Benefits of Unity (Gal. 3:28-29)

In this section Paul affirmed a couple of priceless benefits that we enjoy because we have placed our faith in Christ. Paul brought to the Galatians' attention their status in God's family (3:28) and their inheritance because they belonged to Him (3:29).

In verse 26 Paul brought up believers' status as God's children through faith in Jesus. He then asserted that God erased the distinctions between Jewish and Gentile believers. They didn't need to struggle any longer with the futility of trying to keep the law on their own. They had trusted Jesus Christ to save them. Solely because of their faith in Christ, people in both groups equally belonged in God's family.

But Paul didn't stop with Jews and Gentiles as he described genuine unity in Christ. He went on to include slaves and free people. Slaves represented a distinct class of people who legally belonged to someone else. By contrast, free people considered themselves superior to slaves. Individuals in both social classes were members of the churches of Galatia. In their new status as spiritual siblings in God's family, they could erase the differences in social class that separated them.

Paul took a bold step by insisting that faith in Christ removed class distinctions. He also took a courageous leap by contending that male and female are one in Christ. Back then women generally had little or no power in the world in which they lived. On the other hand, gender gave men a powerful advantage in society. Both male and female believers in Christ, however, have an equal place in God's family.

Granted, being a Christian didn't change anything in a Jewish or Gentile person's family tree. Neither did being saved legally emancipate a slave. Furthermore, receiving Christ didn't erase the obviously different roles for men and women presented in God's Word (see Gen. 1:26-27; 2:18-24). In God's family, however, Christians of different races, social classes, and genders have an equal place.

In God's family, Christians of different races, social classes, and genders have an equal place.

Our status as members of God's family does something else. It assures us of our inheritance. Paul explained earlier that Abraham's faith made him right with God. Furthermore, Abraham's descendents would receive the blessing God promised to him (Gal. 3:6-9). Because we have received Christ by faith, we can see ourselves as Abraham's descendents. Therefore, we will inherit God's blessing.

We have been made heirs of God's blessing by Christ alone. He made the gift possible for us with His sacrifice on the cross. Because of what Christ has done for us, God in His grace gives us the blessing of a relationship with Him that will last for eternity. We will never be excluded from God's family, and we will always be able to enjoy rewarding relationships with our brothers and sisters in Christ.

For Your Consideration

1. How did God break down the walls that separate Christians from one another?

2. What does it mean that all believers are one in Christ? What distinctions have been eliminated, and what distinctions still remain valid?

3. How will you invest yourself in your church in order to strengthen unity among members?

LEARNING ACTIVITY

Breaking Down Walls in Christ

In Galatians 3:28, Paul mentions three human distinctions that were obliterated through the death of Christ and God's offering of salvation by grace and faith alone. In his own experience as a devout Jew, Paul would have prayed each morning and thanked God that He did not make him a Gentile, a slave, or a woman. However, after his conversion, he personally witnessed the power of the gospel breaking through the walls of human division to bring all people together in Christ. Match the references in Acts below to God's redemptive obliteration of human divisions.

Galatians 3:28

1. No Jew or Greek

2. No slave or free
3. No male or female

Salvations in Acts 16

a. Lydia, a dealer in purple cloth from the city of Thyatira, who worshiped God (vv. 11-15)

b. the Roman jailor (vv. 23-34)
c. a slave girl with a spirit of prediction (vv. 16-18)

Answers: 1b, 2c, 3a

The Privilege of Unity (Gal. 4:1-7)

Paul brought the privilege we share as believers into sharp focus by referring to guardians and stewards (4:2). Earlier, Paul compared the law to a guardian who supervised a child's daily activities (3:24). In this section of his letter, however, Paul referred to guardians and stewards as officials who had legal control over a child's money and property. Their control enabled them to deprive the child of any access to his resources until the child became a legal adult. Under guardians' control children had no legal rights. Children had no more power than slaves even though the father had set aside a fortune for the child.

This image of guardians and stewards illustrates the change made in us when we received Christ. Like a father who heaps wealth on his son, our heavenly Father wants to give us eternal life and all the blessings that go along with it. However, just as a guardian deprived a child access to his own wealth, our sin denied us the privilege of a rich and rewarding relationship with God. We lived like slaves who had no choice but to endure our spiritual confinement (4:3).

Yet God released us from our bondage through Christ. God sent His Son under just the right circumstances and at just the right time (4:5). The time was right because of the widespread use of the Greek language, the system of Roman roads, political peace, and the human hunger for a revelation from God. Coming at precisely the right time, Christ redeemed us. He paid the price of His life on the cross so we could be released from our spiritual bondage and given a new life of spiritual freedom. We enjoy the privilege of being God's children, having been adopted into His family because we received Christ (4:4-5).

The image of adoption spotlights God's grace and Christ's purpose in coming. It highlights that salvation is more than forgiveness of sins. Salvation includes a position of blessing and privilege in God's family. As God's adopted children, we have the full privileges of an intimate fellowship with Him and assurance of the fullness of His inheritance.

Being Redeemed

Paul used the dynamic word picture of **redemption** to describe what happened to us when Jesus saved us. In biblical times redemption involved paying the price necessary to secure the release of a convicted criminal. In the Old Testament it also involved property that a person once owned but had lost control of along the way. When the person bought the property back and owned it once again, people would say that he redeemed the property. In the New Testament redemption is one of the ways to describe what Jesus did on the cross. By dying for us, Jesus paid the price necessary to set us free. He bought us back so He could liberate us. (See Rom. 3:24; 1 Cor. 1:30; Gal. 3:13; 4:5; Eph. 1:7.)

Paul gave an excellent portrayal of our intimacy with God in Christ. Think about a three-year-old girl running to her daddy after he has returned home from a long trip. Picture her running toward him with her arms open wide and shouting, "Daddy! Daddy!" That's a fitting picture of what happened to us when Jesus saved us. God's Spirit came to dwell in us when we received Christ, and His Spirit prompts us to embrace our Heavenly Father like an adoring child, crying out, "Abba! Father!" (4:6).

Our salvation leaves us with the blessed assurance that everything changed for us when we trusted Christ. Never again will our access to Him be denied. Now we enjoy the privilege of a relationship with Him that is loving and enriching (4:7).

ILLUSTRATOR PHOTO/ BOB SCHATZ

Left: Manumission (the freeing of slaves) inscriptions at Delphi. Galatians is the Christian's manumission document.

By including us in His family, God has given us a lavish expression of His wonderful grace. Regardless of our background, social standing, race, culture, or gender, we matter equally to Him. All believers have an equal place in His family. Expressed in baptism, our fellowship in Him reflects our unique privilege to be His children. In such a loving relationship, we experience genuine unity with one another as believers.

Regardless of our background, social standing, race, culture, or gender, we matter equally to Him.

For Your Consideration

1. What are the blessings of being a child of God according to Galatians 3:26–4:7? Which blessing of being God's child do you treasure most at the present time? Why?

2. How did Paul define the purpose of Christ's coming in Galatians 4:4-7?

3. Why is adoption such an appropriate picture of the gospel?

Chapter 5
Galatians 4:8-31

BIBLE TRUTH
Freedom from the law is one privilege of being a child of God.

LIFE GOAL
To help you identify the responsibility you have as a result of gaining freedom from the law

CARRYING ON THE FAMILY NAME

Maria got more than she bargained for when she decided to dig into her ancestry. Her family tree hadn't mattered very much to her in the past. However, her interest grew when she helped one of her children with his assignment at school regarding his family tree. Her son's questions about his forefathers led her in search of some answers. However, her research continued long after she helped her son complete his assignment. It soon consumed all of Maria's spare time. She became fascinated with the exploration of her ancestry.

With every fact she uncovered about her family history, she developed a deeper appreciation for her maiden name. She found out that one of her great-great-grandfathers had received a citation for courage under fire when he fought in the infantry. A great-aunt had taken in more than a dozen children during an epidemic that took the lives of their parents. Maria's research made her grateful for the privilege of being a member of such a remarkable family.

Paul feared that the Galatian Christians had lost sight of the value of being in the family of God. In this section of his letter to them, he urged them not to overlook the privilege God had given them to be set free from spiritual bondage so they could become His children.

Because of God's grace we have the privilege of being called His children. By faith in Christ, we become members of God's family. Paul's instruction will enable us to take seriously our responsibility to live in a way that honors our family name.

Resist Returning to the Law (Gal. 4:8-11)

In the Letter to the Galatians, Paul addressed a serious problem involving Christians' leaning toward legalism. The Galatian believers had come to believe that growing toward spiritual maturity meant keeping certain religious rules and ceremonial rituals. By embracing legalism, they appeared to be turning their backs on the precious blessing of spiritual freedom in Christ.

In his effort to encourage the Galatians to stop their drift away from spiritual freedom, Paul contrasted their liberty in Christ to the spiritual imprisonment of legalism. He brought to their attention some basic Old Testament truths. With these truths as his foundation, Paul explained the specific role of the law and underscored God's liberating grace through Christ (3:1-29).

Paul made his argument even more compelling by getting personal with the Galatian believers. He contrasted their past enslavement to idolatry with their present liberty in Christ. Before the Galatians became Christians, they had sold themselves out to the idols of their day (4:8). They had plenty of idols from which to choose a deity to worship. Some of them may have given themselves to worshiping the Roman emperor, while others chose to worship one of the local idols. However, none of the idols they worshiped could actually make their lives better.

None of the idols they worshiped could actually make their lives better.

Furthermore, their service to their dead deities came at a high price. They had to pay the price of honoring the rituals prescribed in the worship of the idols. Doing so meant setting aside certain days of the year for festivals or rituals in order to show their homage. It also meant making costly sacrifices in order to appease the deities to which they had devoted themselves. All in all, it meant being enslaved for life to powerless idols (4:9). Indeed, they paid dearly for serving impotent idols that turned out to be absolutely worthless and meaningless.

Idols in Galatia

Pagan idols abounded in the Galatian region during the time of Paul's missionary journeys. Most likely the apostle had to confront the issue of idol worship often in his work there. For example, the account in Acts 14:8-18 indicates that people confused Paul and Barnabas with two pagan gods. Roman law at that time required the Galatians to worship the emperor. However, plenty of other idols competed with emperor worship. Temples devoted to the worship of Greek gods could be found throughout the region. The presence of the temples there obviously meant that some of the people worshiped Zeus and other mythical gods and goddesses. Other people living in the region apparently paid homage to celestial bodies like the sun, moon, and stars. They believed celestial bodies had the power to manipulate human behavior.

But then Paul came along and preached the good news of Christ in Galatia. God had sent him so they could hear and respond to the gospel. Because of God's initiative, they believed the good news of salvation and gave themselves to Christ. At the moment they received His gift of salvation, God set them free from their spiritual prison. They also became children of God. As members of His family, they could begin to live out their liberty by enjoying the privilege of an intimate walk with Him.

Having been set free from the meaningless service of powerless idols, Paul asked the Galatian Christians why they would be willing to trade in their liberty for legalism, another form of worthless religion. Following the instruction of the Judaizers would once again take them down the sad path toward spiritual imprisonment. They would return to setting aside certain days of the year for prescribed festivals and rituals (4:10). Their lives would be devoted to keeping laws and observing regulations. In essence they would go back to paying a high price for another form of spiritual slavery. No wonder Paul worried about them and feared for their future (4:11).

Christ liberated us from the spiritual bondage of our past when He saved us. Having saved us, He intends for us to make wise choices with our spiritual liberty. Being free in Him doesn't give us permission to live without restraint. Instead He challenges us to see our liberty in Him as a privilege and to live it out responsibly. He placed us in His family so we could fulfill His purpose for our lives. When we embrace a religion of empty rules and rituals, we reflect a lack of wisdom.

For Your Consideration

1. What did Paul say to indicate that God had taken the initiative to save the Galatian Christians?

2. How do Christians today give evidence that they are drifting toward legalism?

3. What steps can you take when you find yourself leaning in the direction of legalism in your walk with Christ?

Below: Overlooking the Temple of Augustus at Antioch of Pisidia. The first-century A.D. temple was built to honor the emperor Augustus. Some of the Galatian believers may have formerly worshiped the emperor.

ILLUSTRATOR PHOTO/ BOB SCHATZ

The Responsibility of Freedom

The freedom believers have in Christ carries with it an accompanying responsibility. Read the verses below and write beside each a responsibility or application.

Galatians 4:8-10 _____

Galatians 4:12-14 _____

Galatians 4:15-16 _____

Galatians 4:19 _____

Galatians 4:29-30 _____

Remember What You First Heard (Gal. 4:12-20)

Paul had a good reason to worry about the Galatian believers. If they continued to drift toward legalism, they would find themselves in a spiritual prison. His worry prompted him to beg them to reconsider their actions. Instead of accepting the disastrous instruction they had been given by the Judaizers, he urged them to follow the example he had set for them. He encouraged them to reconnect with him because of what they had in common with him. The Galatian Christians and Paul shared in common the experience of having placed their faith in Christ and being set free through Him.

We can help one another grow in Christ by setting a worthy example for one another. New believers face challenges in the process of growing in Christ. The stress of these challenges may entice them to give up on the adventure of spiritual liberty in favor of a less stressful spiritual path. The example of a seasoned believer can serve as an anchor to keep a new Christian from drifting in such a dangerous direction.

In Paul's attempt to encourage the Galatian Christians to follow his example, he reminded them of the relationship they once shared. He recalled their kindness toward him years earlier when he traveled to their region to preach the gospel of Christ. The Galatian church had obviously cared for Paul during a time when he suffered from an awful physical problem (4:13-14). Paul may have been suffering with malaria, some sort of eye infection, epilepsy, or something else altogether. We do not know for certain. But in spite of his condition, the Galatian believers took care of him and nursed him back to health. Paul affirmed that their caring attention to him at that time reflected their sacrificial love and sincere appreciation for him (4:14-15).

The Galatians' attitude toward Paul seemed to have changed radically once the Judaizers came into their church. The Judaizers believed simple faith in Christ alone couldn't save anyone. In order to be saved, they insisted that a person needed to be devoted to certain religious rules and rituals from Judaism. They came to the Galatian church with the intention of leading the Christians to follow their heretical instruction.

The Judaizers had to win the trust of the Galatian believers. They apparently accomplished that feat by engaging in an act of deception. They showed their enthusiasm over what the Lord had done in the Galatian churches (4:17). By being enthusiastic, they could win the hearts of the believers. They no doubt also started a smear campaign against Paul in an attempt to destroy his credibility within the churches. Once they discredited Paul, they could build themselves up as legitimate teachers. In turn, they could win the minds of the Galatian Christians.

We identify with Paul when we feel a sense of agony over others' spiritual needs.

Paul was frustrated because he was unable to travel to the Galatian churches himself (4:20). He had no choice but to suffer in anguish over them from a distance. Like a mother-to-be in labor, he already had agonized over them once. When he first met them, his love for them and his eagerness for them to receive Christ made his heart ache for them. He now agonized over them again. This time he ached over their need to serve Christ exclusively and reflect His character in their lives (4:19-20).

We identify with Paul when we feel a sense of agony over others' spiritual needs. Grieving over a friend's need to receive Christ reflects a heart broken for people who need to know Him. Shedding tears when we pray for a lost family member reveals that we understand Paul's burden for reaching people for Christ. Having our hearts broken over brothers and sisters in the Lord

Freedom to Relate

The freedom believers enjoy as a part of God's family of faith liberates them from human constraints. Review the chart below and indicate in the far right column which aspect of our relational liberty in Christ means the most to you and briefly describe why that is the case for you.

Scripture Reference	Constraint from Which Believers Are Liberated	Personal Priority (explain why)
"Become like me, for I also became like you" (4:12).	Not bound by personal perspective only; we can see things from the viewpoint of others.	
"Brothers ... My children" (4:12,19).	Not bound by blood relationships only; bonds based on Christ extend even beyond this life.	
"Though my physical condition was a trial for you, you did not despise or reject me" (4:14).	Not bound by externals or physical liabilities; eyes transformed by grace see more than just the superficial.	
"If possible, you would have torn out your eyes and given them to me" (4:15).	Not bound by personal comfort; believers are free to spend themselves on others, knowing that the life to come is more than adequate compensation for such sacrifice.	
"Have I now become your enemy by telling you the truth?" (4:16).	Not bound by societal convention or human-centered codes of politeness; Christian liberty releases us to seek authenticity in our relationships.	

who take the wrong path also connects us with Paul's agony for the Galatian Christians.

For Your Consideration

1. How did Paul express his anguish and concern for the Galatians?

2. When your heart breaks over another Christian who seems to have given up on walking with God, what do you do about it?

Focus on the Heritage (Gal. 4:21-31)

All of us can probably remember at least one time a devoted friend kept us from making a huge mistake. We may recall how a friend pulled us aside and talked candidly with us. Shooting straight with us opened our eyes and prevented us from doing something we would have regretted later.

As a devoted friend of the Galatian Christians, Paul wanted to prevent them from making a dreadful mistake in their walk with Christ. He knew they hadn't considered all of the facts about the effects of legalism on their spiritual maturity. In order to help them avoid spiritual disaster, he presented the undeniable facts regarding their departure from spiritual freedom and their drift toward a religion of rules and rituals.

Using a portion of the story of Abraham as an analogy, Paul shared some vital facts with them about their heritage as children in God's family. He drew their attention to some compelling details about Sarah and Hagar (Gen. 15-21).

Sarah and Hagar represented the two covenants Paul had brought up earlier (3:15-18). Abraham's wife, Sarah, signified the covenant of God's promise fulfilled in Jesus. Sarah's maid, Hagar, symbolized the covenant on Mt. Sinai in which God gave the law to His people. Accordingly, Sarah represented spiritual liberty in Christ while Hagar represented spiritual bondage to the law. In keeping with the analogy, Paul insisted that the Galatian believers belonged to Sarah, not Hagar.

A CLOSER LOOK

The Story of Abraham as an Analogy

A story in Genesis 15–21 provided Paul with an excellent analogy that he used well in his Letter to the Galatians. Using this analogy, he compared the Old Testament story with the situation facing the Galatian Christians so they could grasp the truth about their place in God's family. The Old Testament account began with Abraham and Sarah's not being able to have any children. However, God promised Abraham that he would have a son. Sarah, Abraham's wife, insisted that he should have a child with Hagar, her maid. After Hagar gave birth to Ishmael, however, God fulfilled His promise to Abraham and Sarah and blessed them with a son named Isaac. In turn, Isaac, not Ishmael, inherited the blessing that God promised to Abraham (Gen. 12:1-3).

With this illustration Paul underscored a convincing fact. Salvation by faith in Christ had placed the Galatian believers in God's family. They shouldn't forget their spiritual heritage. Taking hold of their privilege to be members in God's family would enable them to hang on to the freedom they had been given in Christ and to let go of legalism.

Paul continued to use the analogy to point out two more important facts that the Galatians didn't need to overlook. First, he brought up the sons of the two women and what happened for generations after their births. Hagar's son persecuted Isaac, Sarah's son (4:29). Paul used the analogy to show that people living in spiritual slavery could be expected to trouble Christians who took their spiritual liberty seriously.

Second, Paul highlighted Sarah's son, Isaac, the child of promise (4:23). Granted, Sarah's son had to deal with persecution at the hands of Hagar's son. But he also enjoyed the exclusive privilege of receiving a son's inheritance. Quoting Genesis 21:10, Paul drove home the truth about the inheritance of God's children (4:30). Because the Galatian believers belonged to God's family through Christ, they could count on the same privilege for themselves. However, they needed to reject the teaching of the Judaizers and choose to live in freedom (4:30).

With his analogy Paul presented the pertinent facts about being in God's family. If the Galatians chose a life of keeping religious rules, they would be choosing to ignore the facts about their spiritual family ties. On the other hand, if they decided to live in freedom through Christ, they would be living out the privilege of their heritage as members of God's family.

Paul's analogy helps us to get a better grasp of the blessings we have been given because we received God's gift of salvation. We belong to God's family through faith in Christ. For that reason we are to live like children of God's family. After all, we have been given a most precious privilege.

We can live a life free from the sinful habits and attitudes that once controlled us.

By trusting Christ alone to save us, we also enjoy a new life of liberty. He gives us the unequaled privilege of putting the past behind us so we can look forward to the future. We can live in joyful fellowship with God, honoring Him with our lives.

For Your Consideration

1. What warning did Paul give in 4:30? What does that warning mean for you?

2. What changes do you need to make personally so you can reflect more clearly that you belong in God's family?

Chapter 6
Galatians 5:1-15

FREE TO TAKE A STAND

Eliot couldn't understand why his coach spent so much time teaching the team the right stance for playing football. He envisioned that on his first day of practice he would learn how to block, tackle, throw the ball, and catch it. The coach's obsession with the proper way to stand left him absolutely annoyed. In fact, he considered his first day of practice nothing but a waste of his time.

At the first practice game, Eliot finally understood why his coach took so much time at the beginning on teaching players the proper way to stand. He learned that knowing how to stand was much more than his coach's obsession. It was a fundamental necessity in playing football well. If the players didn't learn how to dig in and take a firm stance, they would lose ground on the football field. Learning the proper stance for the game minimized players' injuring their knees or ankles.

In Galatians 5 Paul called on the Galatians to stand firm. Christ had set them free when He saved them. They must not fall back into the slavery of sin. Taking a stand in freedom implied that they would use their freedom in a way that brought honor to God. Taking a stance was important.

Centuries have separated us from the Galatian Christians of Paul's day. However, the challenge to stand firm in our spiritual liberty remains an equally serious priority for us today. Standing firm in our liberty helps us grow stronger in our walk with Him. It also honors the Lord who gave set us free to serve Him.

Expose Legalism (Gal. 5:1-6)

Paul urged the Galatian Christians to take action by standing firmly against legalism. Choosing an empty religion of meaningless rules and worthless rituals over a dynamic walk with the living Christ would most certainly lead them to disaster. Their faith in Christ had set them free from their slavery to dead deities and coldhearted religion. Embracing legalism would only take them back to the imprisonment of spiritual slavery.

Above: Decumanus in Pisidian Antioch. A decumanus was a major street in a Roman city running east-west. Paul preached in Pisidian Antioch on his first missionary journey (Acts 13:14). Believers there were likely among the recipients of Paul's Letter to the Galatians.

The time had come for the Galatians to take their stand on salvation by grace (5:1). Paul warned them about two serious issues facing them if they caved in to legalism. First, they would be saying that they really didn't need Christ in the first place (5:2). For the Galatian believers the step toward legalism involved submitting to circumcision. If they took such a misguided step, then they would be testifying that Jesus' death didn't have any value after all. They would be insisting that they could save themselves without His sacrifice on the cross.

Second, they would be setting themselves up for greater obligations if they gave in to the demand to be circumcised (5:3). Perhaps they had come to believe that they obligated themselves to do nothing more than practice circumcision. Paul warned them that being circumcised would obligate them to keep every other regulation imposed by the law. Therefore, trying to keep just one regulation would put them back into slavery to the whole law. Consequently, it would be a denial of God's wonderful grace to them by saving them when they placed their faith in Christ.

A CLOSER LOOK

God's People and Circumcision

In the days of the Old Testament, the people of Israel practiced circumcision. God commanded Abraham to circumcise every male in his household and to make sure that his descendents carried out the rite as well (Gen. 17:9-14). Circumcision signified the covenant between God and Abraham and his descendents. Consequently, it marked an Israelite's singular devotion to God. That's why fathers circumcised their infant sons. In due time, however, Moses called on God's people to reflect their devotion to God by circumcising their hearts (Deut. 10:16). Paul insisted that circumcision of the heart meant receiving Christ by faith alone (Rom. 4:9-12).

We must take Paul's warning against legalism seriously. Having been liberated by Christ, we must not make the dreadful mistake of drifting back toward spiritual slavery. Indeed, we have been called to obey the Lord but not in order to pay our way into a personal relationship with Him. We obey Him because He has set us free to enjoy an intimate walk with Him. As a result, we live out the glorious certainty that God's gift of salvation doesn't come by following rules and rituals. Gratitude to Him for saving us by His grace prompts us to obey Him.

God's gift of salvation doesn't come by following rules and rituals.

The sad outcome of legalism cannot be ignored. People who try to work diligently so they can earn the privilege of a relationship with Him ignore God's gift of grace. In so doing, they actually push themselves farther away from Him instead of getting closer to Him. Turning their backs on God's grace, they determine that they will climb the mountain of religious rule-keeping in order to achieve a bond of intimacy with Him. Instead of climbing higher, however, they actually fall farther away from Him by ignoring His gift of salvation by grace.

Incidentally, Paul's statement in verse 4 about falling from grace doesn't imply that we can lose our salvation. In the context of this verse, Paul was contrasting legalism and grace as the basis of Christian life. To fall from grace meant to fall toward a legalistic way of life. His warning to the Galatians was that they not turn their backs on God's sanctifying grace by seeking to relate to Him on the basis of their legalistic acts rather than on the basis of His grace. Choosing to live in legalism would cause them to forfeit the spiritual peace and power for daily living that could be theirs by appropriating God's grace for spiritual growth.[1] Believers impede their growth when they try to mix faith in Christ with an attempt to earn a walk with Him on their own.

For Your Consideration

1. What did Paul mean when he said the Galatians had "fallen from grace" (5:4)?

Left: The Dagger of Gebel al-Arak dates to about 3300-3200 B.C. From Abydos, an ancient city of upper Egypt. The ivory handle, from the tooth of a hippopotamus, is decorated on one side with a scene of war; on the other is a hunting scene. The blade is flint. Circumcision was carried out using a flint knife.

2. Why do some people think they have to work hard at religious duties in order to have favor with God?

3. How do you demonstrate that you have taken your stand for freedom in Christ?

Challenge False Teachers (Gal. 5:7-12)

In the first six verses of chapter 5, Paul encouraged the Galatian believers to stand firm in their spiritual freedom. In verse 7 he turned his attention to the teachers who tried to bewitch them into walking away from freedom. Some false teachers had weaseled their way into the Galatian congregations and attempted to manipulate them. They won the confidence of the churches and proceeded to argue that growing in Christ required believers to work hard at keeping religious rules (4:17-18).

Before the false teachers came into the congregations, Christians in Galatia had made remarkable progress in their walk with the Lord. That's what Paul meant when he told them that they had been running well (5:7). He used the imagery of a footrace to affirm the spiritual growth he had personally seen in them.

Paul showed his disappointment over what had happened to them. Like runners who had been tripped by a devious bystander, the Galatian believers had begun to stumble and fall. Their growth in Christ had been severely hindered. That's why Paul wanted to know who tripped them.

The situation in the Galatian churches shows us how easily false teachers can make their mark on God's people. They come as friends with interesting new insights, but they actually turn out to be devious intruders bent on deceiving Christians with notions that dilute the gospel of Christ. False teachers

The Troublemakers

In Galatians 5:7-12, Paul turned his focus to the false teacher known as Judiazers who had begun to infiltrate the churches of Galatia and teach a "different" gospel (1:6-9). Match the references below to the behavior of the teachers as identified by Paul in verses 7-12.

Reference	Activity
1. Verse 7	a. disturbing
2. Verse 8	b. troubling
3. Verse 10	c. preventing
4. Verse 12	d. persuading

Answers: 1c, 2d, 3b, 4a

generate doubt among believers, polluting Christians' minds and hearts. Following false teachers will stunt a Christian's spiritual growth. For that reason we should guard against false teachers and their poisonous perspectives on the gospel.

Following false teachers will stunt a Christian's spiritual growth.

As Paul warned, just one false teacher can have a devastating influence on entire congregations over time (5:9). Like a small lump of leaven folded into a pan of dough, a false teacher's deceptive instruction can creep into a church. And like bacteria, false teaching can slowly but surely infect one Christian after another. Left unchecked, it will eventually contaminate a church. The potential damage prompts us to heed Paul's warning about the influence of false teachers.

Although disappointed with the work of the false teachers, Paul expressed absolute confidence in the Galatian Christians as they faced the crisis over their freedom in Christ (5:10a). He rested in the assurance that the Lord lived in their hearts. Even though they had been tempted to turn their backs on their walk of faith, the Lord would enable them to resist the temptation.

As for the Judaizers, Paul rested in the assurance that God would hold them accountable for the damage they had done (5:10b). Not only had they deceived the Galatian Christians with their insistence on keeping rules in order to grow in Christ; they had done something else. They had lied about Paul. They had insisted that he also promoted their false instruction.

Nothing could have been farther from the truth. Paul preached the gospel of salvation by God's grace through faith in Christ. His preaching centered on the cross, a message offensive to many (5:11; see also 1 Cor. 1:18,23). Paul's fearless proclamation of the cross got him into trouble everywhere he went. It accounted for the persecution he endured throughout his missionary work. The persecution he endured proved that he preached salvation through faith in Christ alone.

As Paul reflected on the way the Judaizers' lies must have confused the Galatians, his disgust with them intensified. Because of their deceitful lies, the gospel he preached had been compromised, and the believers in Galatia had been confused. Paul registered his disgust with them by challenging the Judaizers to take drastic personal measures in order to validate their wholehearted commitment to legalism (5:12).

For Your Consideration

1. Why is the cross offensive to some (5:11)? How do false teachers sometimes attempt to abolish the cross's offensiveness?

LEARNING ACTIVITY

Leadership Qualities

Paul demonstrated great pastoral leadership when he took a stand against the false teachers in the churches of Galatia. In your Bible look up the verses in Galatians 5 listed in the left column and on the right write a leadership quality you see in that verse.

Verse 7
Verse 8
Verse 9
Verse 10
Verse 11
Verse 12

2. How would you respond if you heard someone say that faith in Christ alone isn't enough to save a person?

Use Freedom Wisely (Gal. 5:13-15)

In these verses Paul brought to the Galatians' attention another crucial concern. They needed to handle their freedom with care. Being irresponsible with their spiritual liberty would be as harmful to them as ignoring it and returning to legalism.

On one hand, we cannot simply ignore our spiritual liberty and obligate ourselves to legalistic rules. On the other hand, we can't abuse our liberty by living however we choose to live. Along with rejecting any form of legalism, Christians need to resist the temptation to turn spiritual liberty into an opportunity to indulge in selfish behavior (5:13). Maturing believers avoid both extremes. We can avoid being swept away in the current of either extreme only by anchoring our freedom in loving service.

Along with rejecting any form of legalism, Christians need to resist the temptation to turn spiritual liberty into an opportunity to indulge in selfish behavior.

In verse 14 Paul explained the relationship between the law and love. Love fulfills the law. In other words,

Christians live out the true intention of the law not by embracing legalism but by loving one another.

Christians live out the true intention of the law not by embracing legalism but by loving one another.

This brings to mind the Great Commandment (Matt. 22:37-40). Paul applied the Great Commandment to his instruction about the right way to put spiritual liberty to work. If we love God, we don't express it by trying to keep empty rules in order to earn His favor. But neither do we display it by abusing our spiritual freedom with self-centered behavior. On the contrary, we show our love for God by loving one another. And we demonstrate our love for one another by serving one another. As we grow in the Lord, we learn to rely on Him to work in us so we can love Him and one another. That's how we live out the authentic intention of God's law.

A CLOSER LOOK

The Old Testament and the Great Commandment

The foundation for the Great Commandment can be found in two Old Testament passages. In Deuteronomy 6:4-5, God instructed His people to show their devotion to Him by loving Him with every fiber of their being. He went on to command His people to love one another as they loved themselves (Lev. 19:18). One day a religious leader asked Jesus to share with him the greatest commandment of all. Jesus replied by quoting both of these passages together (Matt. 22:37-39). Throughout His ministry, He taught His disciples to live according to the commandments He quoted by modeling it for them, ultimately in His death on the cross. In turn, they lived out the Great Commandment in their work. For them, love and not law centered their thinking and guided their actions as they served the Lord.

Paul gave us a glimpse into an apparent problem in the fellowship of the Galatian churches. He hinted that church members were lashing out at one

Left: This Torah scroll dates from the 16th century A.D. It was used in the Spanish Jewish synagogue in the city of Zafed. Christians live out the intent of the Law by loving one another (5:14).

another (5:15). The quarrels could have resulted from the teachings of the false teachers. Their erroneous instruction may have caused a split in the church. Or the biting and devouring could have resulted from something else. No matter what or who caused it, Paul's admonition about loving one another provided the only answer for resolving it. Their strife would destroy the congregation if they didn't address it in love (5:15).

We hurt one another when we fail to love. When we behave selfishly, other believers are victimized, Christian relationships are destroyed, and church unity is threatened. But if we serve one another in love, we will please God with the wise use of our spiritual freedom.

Our freedom in Christ compels us to choose loving service over selfish indulgence.

Paul's instruction about taking a stand encourages us to be wise in the way we use our liberty in Christ. Putting our freedom to good use means exposing the legalism and the threat it poses for us in our spiritual growth. It also calls on us to stand against any teaching that dilutes the gospel message of salvation by grace through faith in Christ. Moreover, our freedom in Christ compels us to choose loving service over selfish indulgence. In these ways we honor God with our spiritual liberty.

For Your Consideration

1. In what ways do Christians today abuse their freedom in Christ (5:13)? How does verse 13 challenge you?

2. What's the connection between the law and loving one another (5:14)?

3. How will you choose to express your love for others through service this week?

---

[1] Max Anders, *Galatians, Ephesians, Philippians, and Colossians,* vol. 8 in *The Holman New Testament Commentary* (Nashville: B&H Publishing Group, 1999), 69.

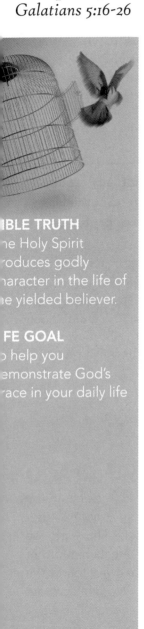

WALK BY THE SPIRIT

Logan and Reid had been friends for a long time. They grew up in the same neighborhood, and they had attended elementary school together. Reid moved away, but he and Logan continued to keep in touch. They enrolled in the same university and graduated at about the same time. In the years that followed, the deep roots of their friendship nourished a healthy and growing bond between their families.

Both Logan and Reid had received Christ when they were little boys, and each of them had grown spiritually. Both grew up with an eagerness to live according to Christian values.

But something strange happened to Logan as he got older. He started to turn a little self-centered. He told Reid that he had made plenty of sacrifices for his family. Now the time had come for him to indulge himself in what he wanted to do.

Concerned about his friend's changing behavior, Reid challenged Logan. He asked, "Logan, doesn't it bother you that you're tarnishing your reputation as a believer? Who's going to believe that you're a Christian?"

Logan replied with an air of arrogance, "Listen, I'm just as much a believer now as when I first got saved!"

"But don't you see that your actions say something entirely different?" Reid countered.

The portion of Paul's letter for this session deals with the problem of selfish behavior. As we will see, it's a spiritual problem that we can resolve as Christians by walking in the Spirit. Walking in the Spirit results in behavior that gives an everyday demonstration of God's grace in our lives.

Hear the Command (Gal. 5:16-18)

When we live out our freedom in Christ responsibly, we provide a vibrant and convincing testimony of God's grace. As we have seen, Paul wanted the Galatians to be aware of two threats to their spiritual liberty. One threat came from believing that growing spiritually required them to practice legalism. The other threat came from thinking they could turn their freedom in Christ into an opportunity for selfish behavior. Both of these threats ignore God's grace.

One threat came from believing that growing spiritually required them to practice legalism. The other threat came from thinking they could turn their freedom in Christ into an opportunity for selfish behavior.

In this part of his letter, Paul focused his attention on the threat of self-indulgence. He addressed the threat by contrasting the Holy Spirit and the flesh. For Paul, the flesh had to do with self-serving behavior that didn't honor Christ. Using the strong language of a command, Paul urged believers to follow the leadership of the Holy Spirit. Being sensitive to the Spirit's leadership would keep them from giving in to the flesh (5:16).

A CLOSER LOOK

Flesh and Spirit

The terms **flesh** and **Spirit** describe the obvious difference between the slavery to selfish urges and the leadership of the Holy Spirit. In the New Testament, the terms work well to show us the stark contrast between the two opposing sources of control in a person's life. A person who gives in to the flesh shows that self-indulgence directs him or her to behave in evil, destructive ways. However, Christians who follow the leadership of the Spirit convey a different message. We demonstrate that the Holy Spirit directs us to behave in productive and fulfilling ways. Because the terms convey the contrast so well, we can understand why Paul used them often in his epistles.

All too often, we find ourselves absolutely powerless to resist the temptation to be self-indulgent in our spiritual freedom. Like opponents in a game of tug-of-war, the flesh constantly tries to wrench us away from the Spirit's control.

When we give in to self-indulgence, we always end up getting irritated with ourselves. Instead of doing what God's Spirit leads us to do, we wind up following the leadership of our self-serving urges (5:17).

The Holy Spirit has the power to help us live out our spiritual freedom in a responsible way. Under His leadership, we can be on the winning course of fulfillment instead of frustration. Getting on the promising course toward spiritual fulfillment, however, requires us to place ourselves at the starting line of dependence. Overcoming the flesh begins by making a bedrock commitment to rely on the power of the Holy Spirit. Making that crucial choice sets us on the path toward spiritual growth in Christ.

Once more Paul addressed the lure of legalism by making a potent assertion about being released from the shackles of the law (5:18). Christians can never count on the law to give them what they need to live in spiritual liberty. The law does not have any power. By contrast, the Holy Spirit alone can empower us so we can live for Christ as people who are truly free.

Growing believers choose wisely to follow the leadership of the Holy Spirit. Making such a wise choice sets us on a course that factors God's grace into our lives. When we place ourselves under the Spirit's leadership, we can count on His power to enable us to live out our freedom in Christ.

For Your Consideration

1. Of what two threats to spiritual liberty did Paul warn the Galatians? Which did he focus on in Galatians 5:16-18?

2. What two things are in conflict in verse 17?

3. What has God provided us to help us overcome evil desires? What is our responsibility in overcoming evil?

The Spirit Versus the Flesh

Read the contrasting references below and fill in each blank.

Spirit
_____ by the Spirit (5:16)
_____ by the Spirit (5:18)
_____ of the Spirit (5:22-23)
_____ to the Spirit (6:8)
_____ life (6:8)

Flesh
_____ the desire of the flesh (5:16)
not _____ the law (5:18)
_____ of the flesh (5:19-21
_____ to the flesh (6:8)
_____ corruption (6:8)

Based on the contrasts Paul drew between the Spirit and the flesh, write an application below that will enable you to "walk in the Spirit" (5:16).

Recognize Ungodly Behaviors (Gal. 5:19-21)

As Paul continued to contrast the flesh and the Spirit, he turned the attention of the Galatian believers to a troubling reality. He described what happened to a person dominated by the flesh by listing some of the disastrous effects of self-indulgence. By studying the list, we can understand that giving in to the flesh will produce a wide range of ungodly behaviors. Self-indulgence will always render devastating effects in the lives of the people who devote themselves to satisfying their own urges.

Paul seemed to arrange his list of ungodly behaviors into four categories. In the first category, he called attention to ungodly sexual practices—sexual immorality, moral impurity, and promiscuity (5:19). These practices are rooted in selfishness. Sexually immoral people tend to see other persons only as a selfish means to an immoral end. The notion of abstaining from a sexual relationship until marriage often is absurd to them.

In the second category, Paul listed two expressions of religious self-indulgence—idolatry and sorcery (5:20). Self-absorbed people garnered temporary satisfaction from worshiping a deity they could touch, see, and control. They also turned to spells and incantations. The exhilaration they experienced from these sources would numb their spiritual pain, at least for a little while.

The third category of ungodly practices strikes at the heart of personal relationships. It includes an extensive list of actions that strike at a person's

relationships (5:20-21). In this rather long list, everything from hatred to envy can be found. These selfish behaviors can lead to the erosion of a friendship, a family, or any other kind of fellowship. People consumed by these behaviors care only about having their way no matter how many relationships get destroyed along the way.

Above: The tell of Derbe (Galatia) in modern Davri, Turkey. Christians in Derbe were likely among the recipients of Paul's Letter to the Galatians.

The fourth category of ungodly practices includes two examples of careless behavior that has gotten out of control (5:21). A person who's drunk portrays a life without restraint. So does an individual who's driven by the consuming need to live constantly in search of the so-called "good life."

Curiously, Paul reminded believers that he didn't provide a complete list ("and anything similar," 5:21). He gave only a few examples of ungodly behavior to be seen in people who were steered by self-indulgence.

As we examine Paul's list, a sobering distinction glares at us. People governed by ungodly behaviors do not reflect the control of the Spirit in their lives. Instead, their urges control them. By contrast Christians rely on the Spirit to help us abhor godless conduct.

The contrast clearly distinguishes Christians from lost people. Those who willfully continue to be characterized by ungodly behavior without any hint of regret or remorse demonstrate their lostness (5:21).

The Kingdom of God

The kingdom of God has to do with the realm of His sovereign rule. Jesus described the kingdom of God in a way that makes it unique. He didn't confine it to a geographical location. Instead, He proclaimed that it existed in the realm of relationships. When we receive Christ by faith, God in His grace welcomes us into His kingdom. As citizens of His kingdom, we enjoy an enriching relationship with Him and with others who have received Christ. Our relationship with Him prompts us to lives as kingdom citizens who reflect the character of Christ in our lives by yielding to the control of His Spirit.

For Your Consideration

1. Into what four categories did Paul arrange his list of ungodly behaviors?

2. How did Paul indicate that this list of ungodly behaviors wasn't complete?

3. Can a person who lives according to the works of the flesh be a genuine believer? Explain your answer.

Exhibit Godly Character (Gal. 5:22-23)

In stark contrast to what happens to a person who gives in to the flesh, Paul explained the outcome of living under the control of the Holy Spirit. When we allow the Spirit to direct us, He works in our lives to produce godly character. We exhibit the fruit of the Holy Spirit's leadership in our lives.

Paul revealed the evidence, or fruit, of a Spirit-controlled life in a list of nine essential character traits that reflect Christ's character in us. Each trait deserves attention in the same way that each individual instrument in an orchestra needs to be tuned properly. But the instruments also need to play together in order to produce music as an orchestra. Just as the sounds of each instrument blend together to produce beautiful music, all of the traits on Paul's list merge together to portray the vibrant character of Christ in our lives. The symphony of Christlike traits pleases our Lord, gives us contentment as we serve Him, and enables people to see Him in us.

Comparing godly character traits to well-tuned instruments playing together in an orchestra helps us in another way. The comparison prompts us to understand the role we play in the process of producing the character traits found in Paul's list. Musicians don't assume that the instruments they play will tune themselves. Rather, they give their instruments whatever attention is necessary in order to render excellent music. In the same way, Christians can't assume that the Holy Spirit works all by Himself to produce godly character in us. We must also take some responsibility for rendering the fruit of the Spirit. As we work under the direction and in the power of the Holy Spirit, the evidence of godly character will become obvious in the way we behave, allowing people to see Christ in us.

The list includes the traits that Christ expects us to exhibit. Jesus exhibited them consistently in His relationships with the Father, His disciples, and anyone else who came in contact with Him. Accordingly, when we follow the empowering leadership of the Holy Spirit, we present a compelling portrait of the love, joy, and peace of Christ. We also exhibit to others His patience, kindness, and goodness. Furthermore, we display His faithfulness, gentleness, and self-control. In these ways we exhibit His character in our lives.

After completing the list of godly character traits, Paul mentioned the law one more time (5:23). He instructed believers to give attention to the fruit of the Spirit but not because a religious law requires us to do so. We strive to let the Holy Spirit control us for one reason alone: we love Christ and want to be like Him.

For Your Consideration

1. What name did Paul give to his list of godly character traits?

2. Which of the character traits listed in 5:22-23 are evident in your life, and which still need more work?

3. What steps can and will you take to reflect the fruit of the Spirit more consistently in your life?

LEARNING ACTIVITY

The Fruit of the Spirit
Galatians 5:22-23

Bible commentators have clustered the fruit of the Spirit into three categories: upward (in relation to God), outward (in relation to others), and inward (in relation to one's self). Match the virtue below with the appropriate category.

1. Love
2. Self-control   a. Upward
3. Faithfulness
4. Patience
5. Peace   b. Outward
6. Goodness
7. Kindness
8. Joy   c. Inward
9. Gentleness

Answers: 1a, 2c, 3c, 4b, 5a, 6b, 7b, 8a, 9c

Left: Entrance lion from Konya, Turkey (biblical Iconium, Galatia).

Follow the Spirit (5:24-26)

As Paul brought the contrast of the flesh and the Spirit to a close, he made a gripping point regarding the Holy Spirit's work in our lives and how we are to relate to the Spirit. His point was drawn from the image of crucifixion.

When crucifixion comes to mind, the ghastly image of Christ's death comes into view. We can see Him hanging on the cross, agonizing in misery on our behalf. Christ's cruel death at Calvary gave us the unparalleled blessing of an intimate relationship with God.

In these verses Paul instructed us to give attention to the image of crucifixion but in another way. Jesus died for our salvation; another crucifixion of that order will never be necessary. At the moment we receive Him as Savior, we belong to Him. Furthermore, our sinful flesh with its desires and passions was nailed to the cross (5:24). We renounced the sinful nature. However, we must see that our conduct conforms to this reality. Ungodly behaviors should no longer be allowed to have control over us.

The image of crucifying the flesh gives us a firm grip on how to live in the Spirit (5:25). Christ gave His life to set us free. In turn, He expects us to surrender our lives to His control. The Holy Spirit lives in us and gives us the power to live godly lives. We must dedicate ourselves to following the Spirit's guidance. Only by following the leadership of the Spirit can we really experience what it means to live in the Spirit.

As Paul drove home the truth about following the Spirit, he instructed the Galatian believers to put it to practical use in their lives. They needed to follow the leadership of the Holy Spirit in ways that would have a positive effect on their fellowship with other believers. They needed to rein in their bad attitudes and selfish conduct. Their self-absorbed conceit would have to go too.

Furthermore, their tendency to provoke one another to bickering and arguing would have to disappear. Likewise, they would have to stop being jealous of one another (5:26).

One evidence of a Spirit-controlled life is the ability to live in harmony with one another.

As believers, we can show in our daily lives many ways that the Holy Spirit controls us. Nothing reflects the empowering leadership of the Spirit in us as does the strong and abiding relationships we nurture with other Christians. One evidence of a Spirit-controlled life is the ability to live in harmony with one another. Christian character is demonstrated by unity with other believers.

Left: In the Church of the Holy Sepulchre in Jerusalem, an altar built over the traditional location of where Jesus' cross stood. Believers identify with Christ in His death and resurrection (2:19-20; 5:24).

ILLUSTRATOR PHOTO/ JAMES MCLEMORE

We tell the story of God's grace through Jesus Christ when we reflect His character in our behavior. When we allow the Holy Spirit to control us, we can expect Him to work in us to produce godly character traits. In turn, we behave in a way that bears witness to the fact that we have experienced God's grace in Christ.

For Your Consideration

1. At the end of Galatians 5, against what things did Paul warn the Galatians to be on guard?

2. How would you summarize the main teaching of Paul in Galatians 5:16-26?

3. What will you do today to give evidence to the fact that you are seeking to walk by the Spirit?

Chapter 8
Galatians 6:1-18

LOVE OTHERS

BLE TRUTH

hristians can
emonstrate God's
race daily by loving
thers consistently.

FE GOAL

help you
emonstrate God's
race in your daily life

After she received Christ, Terri learned that her newfound Lord and Savior expected her to grow in her walk with Him. She took the Lord's expectation seriously and gave herself to the daily disciplines of prayer and Bible study. She shared the good news of Jesus Christ with her family members and friends, and she made serving through her church a priority in her life.

Somewhere along the way, she came to see that the Lord also expected her to reflect His character in all of her relationships. At first she thought that such a lofty challenge obligated her to separate herself from lost people altogether. But she soon discovered that such a path didn't fit her very well.

She talked with some of her friends at church about her dilemma. A seasoned believer named Charlene helped her take a better path. She told Terri, "Show that Jesus lives in you by loving people the way He loves them, the way He loves you."

"How can I do that?" Terri asked.

For the next few minutes, Charlene showed Terri some practical ways to put her love for Christ to work in her relationships with others. She also encouraged Terri to love people in Christ's name even though they may not respond by loving her in return.

In the same way, Paul taught the Galatian Christians how to reflect God's grace to them by loving others consistently and unconditionally. As we study this passage, we will encounter the everyday expressions of God's loving grace that He expects us to exhibit in our daily lives.

Help Carry Others' Loads (Gal. 6:1-5)

Demonstrating Christ's love to people leaves us gratified when they love us in return. However, Paul enjoined the Galatian believers to love people whether or not they responded lovingly. Loving people even when they don't love us in return sets us apart as God's people. It reflects His grace in saving us through faith in Christ alone.

In these verses Paul showed us a way to put God's love to work in our relationships with other Christians. We sometimes face the sad reality of a spiritual brother or sister falling into sin. Our natural reaction to such a reality may be to turn our backs on a believer who has brought shame on the body of Christ.

But we are challenged to take a different approach. Instead of casting aside a Christian who has fallen into sin, Paul urged believers to reach out to him or her. With the goal of reconciliation, we should try to restore a fallen Christian with gentleness.

Without condoning sinful conduct, we are to make the effort to bring a broken believer back to spiritual health. The word "restore" in verse 1 means "to mend," as in mending a net or setting a broken bone. Healing may take time, and it may require us to make a series of sacrificial investments in the person. But it's worth the effort when we consider the fact that we aren't immune from slipping down the slope of temptation either.

Pride can get in the way of restoration if we're not careful (6:3-4). Pride can prevent us from reaching out to help other believers. Likewise, the pride of a

Fulfilling the Law of Christ

"Carry one another's burdens; in this way you will fulfill the law of Christ." Galatians 6:2

Read Galatians 6:1-5. Fill in the blanks below and write an action step to apply that truth.

1. Believers fulfill Christ's commandment to love one another when they _____ someone who has fallen into sinful behavior.
   Application:

2. Those who attempt to restore fallen believers should themselves be _____.
   Application:

3. Pride is the attitude when people think they are something when they are _____.
   Application:

4. Believers should help one another carry their heavy burdens, but all believers have to _____ their own work and then carry their own _____.
   Application:

Answers: 1. Restore; 2. Spiritual; 3. Nothing; 4. Examine and Load

believer who has fallen can prevent him or her from either asking for or accepting help from other Christians. Sometimes believers who have fallen don't think they need or even deserve any help.

Notice that Paul made a clear distinction between "burdens" and "load" in this portion of his letter. On one hand, he insisted that believers should help a brother or sister in Christ who is carrying a burden that's absolutely too heavy to bear alone (6:2). On the other hand, God holds us responsible for carrying our own

Left: The tell of Lystra near the Turkish village Khatyn Serai. Lystra was located in Galatia. Paul visited there on his first and second missionary journeys (Acts 14:8-20; 16:1-2).

load of personal responsibility for our lives (5:5). Some burdens are so heavy we need help in carrying them. Other loads are our responsibility alone to carry. In this context the "burdens" mentioned in verse 2 primarily refer to the believers caught in sin.

For Your Consideration

1. What responsibilities do Christians have for one another according to these verses?

2. Paul instructed the Galatians to carry one another's burdens (6:2), then he told them that each person must carry his own load (6:5). Explain why this is not a contradiction.

Loving Others

Read each verse below and answer the questions either True or False.

1. Verse 1: When other believers fall into sin, we should leave
   them alone.   T or F
2. Verse 1: We show love when we are gentle with others.   T or F
3. Verse 2: We love others when we let them carry life's burdens alone
   and learn fortitude.   T or F
4. Verse 5: We love others when we encourage and empower them
   to take responsibility for their own load in life.   T or F
5. Verse 3: We have to deal with pride before we can truly give or
   receive love.   T or F
6. Verse 6: We love God's leaders by sharing financially with them.
                                                                T or F
7. Verse 9: We should offer love to people once or twice but stop if they
   reject it.   T or F
8. Verse 10: We love everyone but pay special attention to fellow
   believers.   T or F

Answers: 1F, 2T, 3F, 4T, 5T, 6T, 7F, 8T

Spread Godly Works (Gal. 6:6-8)

In these verses Paul revealed another way to put love to
work in our relationships with other Christians. This
example strikes at the heart of an important kingdom
task: teaching God's Word so believers can grow in
Christ.

The Galatian Christians had benefited from Paul's
instruction when he stayed with them. Devoting himself to their spiritual growth by teaching them was a
labor of love for him and a source of spiritual blessings
for them. Apparently, Paul never expected the believers
to pay him for his work as a teacher. But he expected
them to give generously to support other Christian
teachers whom God would send to them (6:6).

In keeping with Paul's directive, discerning Christians

**Left: Roman aqueduct
at Pisidian Antioch
(Galatia). Paul preached
in Antioch of Pisidia
on his first missionary
journey (Acts 13:14).**

express their love for teachers and other leaders who faithfully instruct them in God's Word. Pastors and other ministers who give their lives to the growth of believers deserve respect and appreciation. Our financial support of their ministries speaks volumes about our gratitude to God for them. When we share financially with ministers who turn our attention to God's Word, we enable them to carry on their work of making disciples. Also, we participate in the important kingdom task of helping believers grow spiritually through faithful instruction in God's Word.

Paul warned that we can't fool God. God knows if we ignore our obligation to help other believers. God clearly sees the kinds of seed we sow. We can rest assured that the harvest we reap will be in keeping with the seeds we have planted (6:8). Granted, the harvest may not come soon. In fact, we may not be able to see the harvest of our investment for some time. Even so, the harvest will come. That's when a person who sows selfishness will reap a harvest of spiritual devastation. By contrast, a Christian who invests in God's work can count on reaping eternal rewards.

A CLOSER LOOK

Mocking God

Paul used a Greek word for **mock** that he never used in any of his other epistles. In fact, the word doesn't appear anywhere else in the rest of the New Testament. The Greek word denotes a person who turns up his or her nose at someone in a show of mockery and contempt. The word paints a verbal picture of deviant individuals who turn their noses up to God as a sign of their disrespect of Him and their resentment of His authority in their lives.

Paul's assertion about sowing and reaping both troubles us and encourages us at the same time. On the one hand, it presents the sobering reminder that people who indulge in their selfish urges will eventually face God's judgment. When judgment day comes, they can only expect eternal destruction because they turned their nose up at God's grace in Christ Jesus. On the other hand, it encourages believers to remember God's promise. When we follow the leadership of God's Spirit, we can expect to enjoy the spiritual fulfillment that life in Him has in store for us. In that way we see the principle of sowing and reaping at work in a positive way.

We must habitually do good works even when we don't see an immediate result.

For Your Consideration

1. What will be harvested from sowing to please the sinful nature?

2. How does engaging in self-indulgent behavior mock God?

3. What are your plans for affirming your Bible teacher's faithfulness in instructing you in God's Word?

Keep On (Gal. 6:9-10)

Christians can grow weary from serving God (6:9). The weariness may result from doing kingdom work for a long time without seeing any visible results of our efforts. Days can turn into weeks, which eventually turn into years and perhaps decades, and still we don't see much of a harvest. Our frustration is compounded by our observation that relatively few believers appear to be joining us in the work to be done. Even though a large number of believers say that they want to participate in kingdom work, only a handful actually show up when the time comes to get involved. Over time our frustration can make us want to throw up our hands and quit.

Christians can grow weary from serving God.

We can rest in the certainty that a harvest will come in due time (6:9). Perhaps we will see it not long after we invest ourselves in others. However, many years may pass before we see the outcome of our acts of loving service. We may not see it until we get to heaven. Ultimately, that's where we will see once and for all the fruit of our labor in Christ. Then we'll see that all of our efforts were worthwhile and that our time wasn't wasted. In the presence of Jesus, we will know that it all was worthwhile. So until we reap the harvest, we can't let ourselves give up on the kingdom work to be done.

Instead of waiting around idly for the harvest to come, we are to keep on looking for opportunities to do good to all people (6:10). Paul stated clearly that our love should be directed to all people everywhere. God created every person, and He loves each one of them immensely. In His love He sent His Son to die for each and every one of them.

We love them regardless of how they respond to us. We do good to them by being kind to them, caring for them, praying for them, nurturing relationships with them, and sharing the gospel of Christ with them. Many of them may not respond to the gospel, but our love for them won't allow us to exclude them from hearing it.

Paul also urged us to give particular attention to caring for one another in the fellowship of believers. The Great Commission calls on us to reach out to lost people outside the church. But we cannot overlook the need to care for one another as we carry out this ambitious assignment. As we grow stronger together, we are more capable of expressing Christ's love to others in order to reach them for Christ. When we build up one another in His love, we make a difference in the way we carry out kingdom tasks together.

For Your Consideration

1. According to Galatians 6:9-10, when should Christians try to do good to people, especially fellow believers?

2. What causes a believer to grow weary of serving in Christ's name? What encouragement did Paul offer to weary Christians?

3. Which of your Christian friends needs your encouragement because he or she has grown weary in work of serving the Lord?

Follow Paul's Example (6:11-16)

The letter to the Galatian Christians has given us some insights into the reach of Paul's love and the depth of his burden for them (6:10). When we read that he wrote in large letters to them (6:11), we imagine how he expressed his passion for them with oversized print. Granted, he may have written in large letters because he couldn't see very well. Or maybe he wanted to ensure his friends in Christ of the authenticity of the letter. They didn't have to wonder if the letter had been forged by one of his adversaries. However, the large letters in his own handwriting certainly remind us of his intense passion for them and their growth in Christ.

The evidence of Paul's passion can also be seen in what he challenged the Galatian believers to do with their spiritual freedom. With the letter almost at an end, he appealed to them one last time to follow his example of complete devotion to Christ.

Paul urged the Galatians to embrace the cross.

In particular, Paul urged the Galatians to embrace the cross. The Judaizers who had come into the Galatian churches tried to avoid the cross because of the persecution associated with proclaiming it. By instructing the believers in Galatia to be circumcised in order to grow in Christ, the Judaizers showed that they wanted to promote a safe path to spiritual growth. They also wanted to boast over the way they persuaded the Galatian Christians to walk away from God's grace by taking the route of religious legalism (6:11-13).

In contrast Paul testified that he didn't run from the cross of Christ at all. Instead, he embraced it passionately. For that reason he refused to boast about anything other than the cross (6:14). Any interest in trying to take a safe route toward spiritual maturity died when he gave his life to Christ. In view of what Christ had done for him, nothing else mattered to him. Being a new creation in Christ meant more to Paul than simply being a religious person devoted to legalism (6:15).

Because of what Christ has done in us when He saved us, we can echo Paul's powerful testimony. We belong to the people of God and experience His peace and mercy. These blessings reflect His wonderful grace to us through Christ (6:16).

A CLOSER LOOK

The Israel of God (6:16)

Paul used this term "the Israel of God" only in his epistle to the Galatians. Although Bible scholars haven't settled on Paul's exact meaning of the term, they have called attention to some unique clues provided by the broad context of the Galatian letter. An important clue can be found in the fact that Paul shows us how Christians are descendents of Abraham through Jesus Christ. Consequently, we belong to Israel in a spiritual sense. God's Israel is composed of people who have received His gift of salvation through faith in Jesus Christ.

Paul words at the end of his letter leave us with a compelling image of his devotion to Christ. The marks in Paul's body told a story of his willingness to

ILLUSTRATOR PHOTO/ JERRY VARDAMAN COLLECTION

go the distance because of the cross. Laying our lives on the altar of sacrifice to Christ tells the same story of our undying devotion to Him (6:17-18).

We are grateful to the Lord for leading Paul to write about ways to express God's love to other people. In this final chapter we have learned how we can fulfill the Great Commandment by loving the people Christ died to save. Our care for other believers expresses our willingness to put our spiritual freedom to work for His glory. Going the distance by helping broken believers, encouraging teachers of God's Word, sowing seeds of love, and devoting ourselves to Christ alone reflects that we have embraced the truth about God's grace to us.

For Your Consideration

1. How had the Judaizers been hypocritical in their relationship with the Galatian Christians?

2. How is being a new creation in Christ different from simply being a devoutly religious person?

3. In light of this study of Galatians, how can you demonstrate God's grace in your life?

Left: Gleaning grain in Israel. Paul taught that the harvest we reap will be in keeping with the seeds we have sown (6:8).

Two Ways to Earn Credit
for Studying LifeWay Christian Resources Material

CHRISTIAN GROWTH STUDY PLAN

CONTACT INFORMATION:
Christian Growth Study Plan
One LifeWay Plaza, MSN 117
Nashville, TN 37234
CGSP info line 1-800-968-5519
www.lifeway.com/CGSP
To order resources 1-800-485-2772

Christian Growth Study Plan resources are available for course credit for personal growth and church leadership training.

Courses are designed as plans for personal spiritual growth and for training current and future church leaders. To receive credit, complete the book, material, or activity. Respond to the learning activities or attend group sessions, when applicable, and show your work to your pastor, staff member, or church leader. Then go to *www.lifeway.com/CGSP*, or call the toll-free number for instructions for receiving credit and your certificate of completion.

For information about studies in the Christian Growth Study Plan, refer to the current catalog online at the CGSP Web address. This program and certificate are free LifeWay services to you.

Need a CEU?

CONTACT INFORMATION:
CEU Coordinator
One LifeWay Plaza, MSN 150
Nashville, TN 37234
Info line 1-800-968-5519
www.lifeway.com/CEU

Receive Continuing Education Units (CEUs) when you complete group Bible studies by your favorite LifeWay authors.

Some studies are approved by the Association of Christian Schools International (ACSI) for CEU credits. Do you need to renew your Christian school teaching certificate? Gather a group of teachers or neighbors and complete one of the approved studies. Then go to *www.lifeway.com/CEU* to submit a request form or to find a list of ACSI-approved LifeWay studies and conferences. Book studies must be completed in a group setting. Online courses approved for ACSI credit are also noted on the course list. The administrative cost of each CEU certificate is only $10 per course.